HOW TO SURVIVE IN STYLE

HOW TO SURVIVE IN STYLE
by
Carolyn A. Gelderman

To order more copies:

How To Survive in Style
PO Box 281
West Byfleet, Surrey KT14 6PG

My thanks to Sheila Millard, Alice Russell and
Janet Wilmoth for their assistance and
encouragement in the preparation of this book.

Copyright 1985 Carolyn A. Gelderman
ISBN 0 9510278 0 8
Edited by Elizabeth R. Krijgsman
Illustrations by Veronica A. Kelly
Printed by Perfectaprint, Byfleet, Surrey
Although every effort has been made to ensure accuracy, the author
cannot assume any responsibility for possible errors in the
information included.

Contents

CHAPTER 1

How To Find a House

HOW TO SELECT THE GENERAL AREA

The first place to look when starting your house-hunting is not out there at all that real estate, but into your own heart. There lies the answer to the first and most basic question: am I a City Mouse or a Country Mouse?

The City Mouse

If you are a City Mouse, you will have London at your feet. The best of the world's theater and dance performances are within half an hour's drive, and history is just around the corner in the form of that blue plaque denoting a house of historical interest. You are temptingly close to the most exciting shopping — Harrod's Food Halls will deliver to your doorstep, you can easily make it to the first day, not to mention the first hour, of the January and July sales, and you can buy your appliances at the John Lewis stores, who boast the lowest prices anywhere. Although you may not own a single blade of grass yourself, there are parks galore, with ducks to feed, open-air concerts to attend, and even lakes to boat on!

You must be a realistic City Mouse, however, and consider the following drawbacks: owning a car will bring the frustrations of traffic jams and the lack of parking spots, and you will have to get used to taking buses and the Underground; rents are high, and chances are that you will find yourself in an apartment; your younger children will need your supervision every time they go out the front door. Don't be fooled into thinking that a house in London will automatically solve the commuting problem for all members of the family, because a commute across the city can take as long as a train ride in from the country.

Areas of London for the City Mouse

Now get out your city map and pencil and consider the following areas, preferably while having yourself driven around London.

There are 32 boroughs in London, and although some are just too seedy or too posh to be considered home, remember that each borough is like a separate village and has all types of housing — the sophisticated borough with its while-pillared houses will also contain apartments, and detached houses will be scattered among elegant blocks of flats.

St. John's Wood (NW8) is just north of Regent's Park and within walking distance of the American School of London. Flats, detached houses, and row houses with gardens are all available. This·area is convenient, popular, pleasant, and therefore expensive.

Hampstead (NW3), just north of St. John's Wood, is the place for the City Mouse with a bit of the Country Mouse in her soul. You can walk for miles on Hampstead Heath and still get to the West End theaters in 20 minutes.

Holland Park (W11, W14) is just east of Hyde Park and has its very own park, as the name implies. Less bustling than Kensington and Chelsea and less expensive than Belgravia, it has a good mix of detached and row (*terraced*) houses and many flats, making it a nice place for a family.

Kensington, Chelsea, and Fulham (SW3, SW5, SW6, SW7, SW10, W8), together form a large area extending south of Hyde Park and Kensington Gardens to the Thames. You will find a nice combination of bustling shopping streets (King's Road, Fulham Road, and Kensington High Street) and an oasis of peace in the residential streets and private fenced parks, often with tennis courts. Many of the roomier townhouses have been converted into flats.

Knightsbridge (SW7, SW1), just south of Hyde Park, offers quiet, expensive housing in the midst of some very luxurious shopping, such as Harrods with its seductively convenient Food Halls. There are apartments and Georgian row houses surrounding those charming squares.

Regent's Park (NW1) lies around the park of the same name. Here you find luxurious houses, including Winfield House, the residence of the American Ambassador. The London Zoo, a short walk away, is an ideal Sunday afternoon activity.

Belgravia (SW1), a small area west of Buckingham Palace and south of Hyde Park Corner, is a rich cousin to Kensington, as its elegant Regency houses show. Lining narrow cobblestone streets, the mews houses (converted stables and coach houses) are more affordable.

Mayfair (W1), east of Hyde Park, is an area of fine restaurants, hotels, clubs, and antique shops. Few houses are available, but it is the perfect place to find an elegant apartment.

The Country Mouse

If, looking into your heart, you see a Country Mouse, then you will be looking at houses in some of the prettiest countryside imaginable. You will hear the foxes playing at night, with their babylike cries, and you'll drive along picturesque winding roads lined with hedgerows just to get to the dentist. You may be able to afford a larger house with more lawn than you'll want to mow, English Country neighbors, despite their reputation for initial chilliness, will be responsive to an informal invitation for a glass of sherry.

The Country Mouse, however, has to live with certain drawbacks: a trip to London, even though it's no more than 20 miles away, remains quite an undertaking. Your car will become your second home, and some days will find you crawling into it five times at least, as you fetch, carry, haul, drop off, and pick up. For special items, from Greek recipe ingredients to a new hat for the Ascot races, you may have to go into London.

The vital consideration among all those mentioned above may well be the question of schools. (For a discussion of this question, turn to Chapter 2.) The ideal spot to live is that perfect point where transportation to job, proximity to school, and that affordable dream house all converge.

Areas of the Country for the Country Mouse

The Country Mouse has all the freedom and the frustration that too much choice brings. Your first task, then, is to narrow your choices by considering the three most important factors: the type and price of housing available; train service to your breadwinner's job; location and transportation to schools. Study these two maps until you know them like the palm of your hand.

Surrey

Cobham is the home of the American Community School (ACS), and its houses (and rent levels) reflect this fact. The nearest train station is Stoke d'Abernon.

Oxshott and Stoke d'Abernon are adjacent to Cobham; both have train stations.

Esher is nicely situated — close to ACS and a very short train ride away from Waterloo Station. The High Street, the old A3 to London, tends to be congested.

Walton-on-Thames offers two housing estates, Ashley Park and Burwood Park. There is good train service to London and bus service to ACS and the TASIS school in Thorpe.

Weybridge includes St. George's Hill and Oatlands Village. The center offers practical shopping; there is good train service to

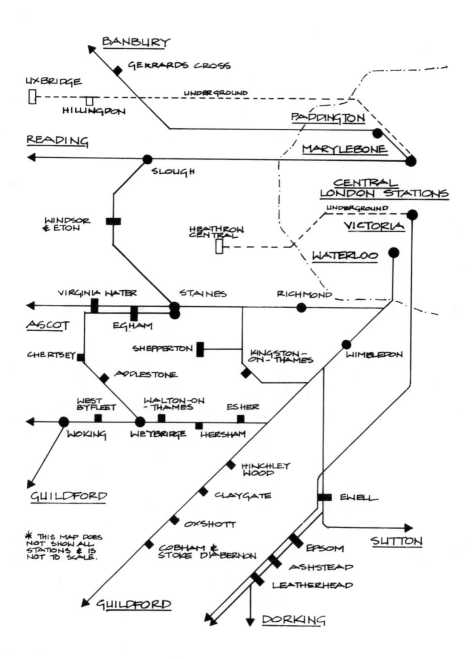

Train Service for the Country Mouse

Waterloo Station and bus service to ACS and TASIS.

Woking, although farther from London than some other Surrey towns, is very close to London by train: its direct nonstop rail service is excellent. The Canadian School is located here. Look into The Hockering and Hook Heath areas.

West and East Horsley are farther into the Surrey countryside, with bus services to ACS.

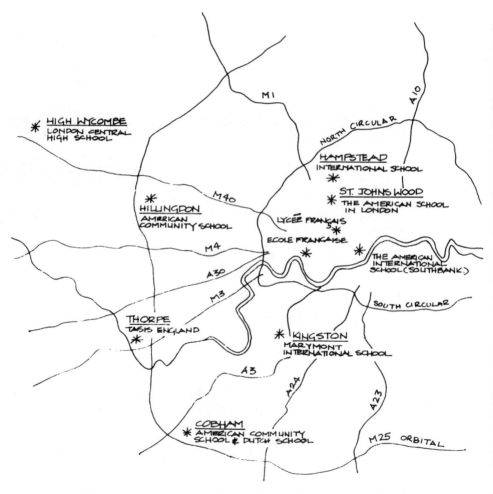

Non-British Schools

Leatherhead, a sizeable town, is surrounded by smaller towns and villages, such as Ashtead and Bookham, offering lovely housing.

Richmond, Kingston and Wimbledon (SW14, SW19, SW20) are on the edge of London and therefore combine the best features of city and country life. These villages are international in flavor thanks to the foreign schools in the area. From Wimbledon and Richmond there is Underground service into London.

Berkshire (say BARKshur)

Ascot, Sunninghill, Sunningdale, and Virginia Water
These picturesque commuter towns to the west of London are conveniently located — close to Heathrow (but with little air traffic noise) and the TASIS school in Thorpe. Although the train service to London is less direct than from Surrey towns, you are in a web of highways (the M3, M4, and M25).

Buckinghamshire

Gerrards Cross and Beaconsfield (say JERrards and BECKonsfield)
Both towns, northwest of London, are relatively close to the American Community School in Hillingdon and have good train service to the American School of London. Housing ranges from the modern development to the old brick mansion. The location makes it easy to explore most of England without the hassle of first getting through or around London

HOW TO FIND AND USE A REALTOR

The woman wearing rose-colored glasses and spouting superlatives is your **realtor** *(estate agent)*. She makes her money by selling or renting houses and charging the owner around 2% for her services when you buy and 10% when you rent. She therefore represents him, and not you. She has your best interests at heart only to the extent that they coincide with hers — and hers is to sell or rent the property at the highest possible price in the shortest possible time. Don't disregard her, though, since she can help in certain ways:

She has **listings** of properties for sale or rent in her area, arranged according to price, which she will send you free of charge. One listing may cover two whole pages and will include room measurements and often a photograph. Read all the particulars carefully to sharpen your feeling for prices in your range and geographical area. Learn to read this jargon and to sift through the superlatives. Although the realtor is not allowed to misrepresent the qualities of a property, these descriptions are in no way legally binding. Although houses can be listed with several realtors, there is no official multiple listing service, so you will have to deal with several agents in order to make sure you get to see all available properties.

Like some sort of matchmaker, **the realtor will set up an appointment for a viewing** but may not accompany you. The owner will show you through the house himself, which means you have to listen to his sentimental reminiscences and use sign language to communicate with your spouse. If the house is vacant, you may be given a key or the estate agent will accompany you.

The realtor will act as intermediary between you and the vendor or leasor once you've found the house of your dreams. In the case of a sale property, she will **take your deposit** and lead you through the complicated dance-steps that follow (see *How to Buy a House,* further on in this chapter). In the case of a rental property, she now begins the hardest part of her job, conveying your requests to the owner and bringing his arguments about the impossibility of your demands back to you. The house is by no means yours at this time, so be flexible.

There is no law to prevent anyone from hanging up a real estate shingle and starting to show houses, but you can narrow the field of suitable realtors in a few ways. First of all, read the housing ads in several newspapers (the *Sunday Times,* the *Evening Standard,* and the *Times,* for example), to see which agents are mentioned often, which area they operate in (remember, there is no multiple listing service), and what type of housing they have to offer. Choose an agent that has taken the trouble to join one of the professional societies, which will at least guarantee the safety of your deposit. Look for these initials after the agents' names: RICS, ISVA or NAEA. Rental agents have their own association: ARLA.

In your wanderings, write down the names of agents that appear on signs in front of houses you would consider. Form your own list using this approach in combination with the listing in the Yellow Pages under Estate Agents.

RELOCATION AGENTS

In these shark-infested waters, you may have one lifesaver in the form of an understanding relocation agent. Her services are paid for by the company your breadwinner works for, so she is working for you, dealing with more than one realtor. She is an excellent source of information on everything from schools to grocery shops to local sports facilities, so pump her for all she's worth while you're in her car and she can't escape.

Although she is usually hired by a company, you can also engage her services yourself, by contacting one of the relocation offices:

International Relocation Company Ltd.
92 New Cavendish Street
London W1
tel. 01-631 1944

Merrill Lynch Relocation Managements Ltd.
87 – 91 New Bond Street
London W1
tel. 01-629 8222

Roots Relocation
Mrs. Anna Adam
"Roots"
Dartnell Avenue
West Byfleet, Surrey
tel. Byfleet (09323) 41846

HOW TO VIEW A HOUSE

Whether you rent or buy, whether you're a City Mouse or a Country Mouse, train those beady eyes on the properties you consider. The estate agent represents the property owner and not you; therefore you must be as wary and critical as when confronted with any salesman.

The Kitchen

The English country kitchen often has space for table and chairs or adjoins a breakfast room. You can expect the following appliances: a stove *(cooker)*, either gas or electric, with an eye-level broiler *(grill)*. The stove top is called the *hob;* the oven, or maybe two ovens, may be built in. Even if there is no dishwasher, look for water and drain hook-ups. Most dishwashers heat their own water, instead of drawing it from the main hot-water supply. This has the obvious advantage of not using up the hot water right before evening baths, but the disadvantage of a very long wash cycle.

There may not be a separate laundry room; don't be surprised to find your washing machine in the kitchen, and don't be surprised if there is no accompanying clothes dryer. Lack of sun and abundance of rain makes a clothes dryer a necessity, so negotiate this matter with your landlord.

Because houses with cellars are rare, the furnace *(boiler)* may also be in the kitchen. This is not a sooty black monster but a modest white appliance that fits under your kitchen counter and looks like just another appliance. It heats water for the radiators as well as all the faucets *(taps)*.

The refrigerator may be smaller than you're used to, so consider a second refrigerator somewhere else in the house (or garage). Don't expect a garbage disposal or a microwave oven.

The Bathroom

Check the heating and the plumbing. Is the heated towel rail the only source of heat? Although there will be a good-sized bathtub, there will not always be a shower head above the tub. And even if there is, it is apt to be the hand-held, detachable kind; even worse, it will probably emit a feeble stream of water similar to a light summer mist. The reason for this is that your water is stored in the tank under the roof and falls (is not pumped) from there by the force of gravity. For some inexplicable reason, this means that water absolutely gushes out of the faucet in the tub and trickles out of the shower head! The greater the vertical distance between the tank and the faucet, the greater the water pressure. One solution is to install a pressure pump — one for each shower.

The toilet (and maybe bidet) will probably be in the bathroom; if not, look for a separate cubicle down the hall, designated as the w.c. (you may refer to it as the "toilet" or the "loo"). A bathroom that does not contain a tub is usually called a shower room; this is often a converted closet off the master bedroom. It is illegal to have an electrical outlet in the bathroom, except the special one for a shaver.

Don't assume that every bedroom will be accompanied by its own bathroom. You'll be looking at houses with only one and can count yourself lucky if you find a place with two. As they say, most English houses are long on gardens and short on bathrooms.

The living room *(lounge, sitting room)*

Check the fireplace; the glowing fake fire is probably removable, and in back of it you may find an attractive, if shallow, fireplace that actually takes logs. Fireplace wood is difficult to locate because everyone seems to have a private supply, but, come fall, try garden centers and greengrocers. Because of the Clean Air Act, the City Mouse is not allowed to burn logs. Buy smoke-free fuel that looks like charcoal briquets instead. The house that boasts a *baxi-grate* has an easy-to-clean fireplace grate with a drawer that catches the ashes and can be emptied easily — sometimes even from outside the house!

The Dining Room

If separate from the living room it often has a pass-through or serving hatch from the kitchen.

The Bedrooms

Check the storage; there may be no built-in closets, particularly in smaller bedrooms. Buy free-standing cupboards *(wardrobes)* or, in case of a surplus of bedrooms, designate one as a walk-in closet and dressing room.

Because most houses lack basements and attics and the storage space they offer, don't forget, when considering the minimum number of bedrooms you require, to set one aside for general storage.

You may find a bedroom with a washbasin in it; value this, because it is a tremendous help in alleviating the congestion in the too-few bathrooms.

Again, check the heating. An unheated bedroom is not unusual in England and electric heaters *(space heaters)* are a common sight, especially in apartment buildings with communal heat that is turned off in the summer.

GLOSSARY OF TERMS FOR THE HOUSE MOUSE

The realtor's jargon is very different from every-day English as we all know it. Remember, her loyalty is to the present owner of the house, whether she is renting or selling to you, and if she can possibly praise a feature, she will. If she hasn't mentioned it, it either doesn't exist or is sadly deficient.

Study the following alphabetical list of terms as you would a vocabulary list in a foreign language:

The **airing cupboard** can be found in the upstairs hallway, warm and cozy from the water heater hiding there. Use it as the English do, to store your linens and to lay out damp things, like wet mittens or bathing suits, for quick drying. Try unconventional uses, too: set bread dough to rise, make yoghurt, dry flowers.

An **aspect** is an outside wall offering a view. A room with a double aspect has two outside walls, both with windows; a west-backing aspect means an outside wall with windows facing west, and a northern aspect is cold.

A **block of flats** is an apartment building, originally built for just that purpose *(purpose-built block)*. A *mansion block* is older and probably more spacious.

The **boiler** is your furnace, using either oil or natural gas *(oil- or gas-fired)*, and is often found in the kitchen.

Volumes could be written on **central heating** and the British attitude toward this "new-fangled" idea, so be wary. Check the furnace *(boiler)* which probably uses natural gas and most likely stands in the kitchen; check the thermostat, often a dial with a timer allowing you to adjust the heat according to the hours of the day; and most certainly not least, check the size and number of radiators. Look for double radiators, which give off more heat. An unheated bedroom or bathroom is not as rare as you might hope!

A **cloakroom**, a small room off the front hallway, often does double duty. It contains the coat hooks (hence its name) and the toilet. In public places, ask for the cloakroom instead of the ladies' room.

A **company let** means that your employer signs the rental agreement in your stead. Many landlords mistakenly believe that this prevents early termination of the lease when you move. This and other misconceptions have been set straight in the Rent Act 1977 and the Housing Act 1980.

A **cooker**, aptly named, is the kitchen stove, either gas or electric. The cooking surface, or burners alone, is termed the *hob*.

Coving, a strip of wood at the angle where the wall meets the ceiling, is considered a desirable feature.

A **cul-de-sac** or **close** is a dead-end street.

A **crazy paved footpath** is a very sane flagstone path.

Double glazing is a double layer of window glass, a great conserver. The layers may look like a single layer, or the second layer may simply be screwed on to the existing window frames on the inside. *Double glazing,* together with *cavity fill,* a polyester insulation between two external walls, will reduce the heating bill.

Electric points are electrical outlets. If they and their matching plugs look large and clumsy, remember that much of the bulk is safety protection against the powerful voltage (240 volts).

Elevation indicates not the height but the front, or facade, of a house.

An **extractor hood** above your stove contains a fan to draw off cooking odors. It probably has no outside outlet, so you need to change the filter every six months.

A **fitted kitchen** contains built-in appliances and matching wall and floor cupboards.

Fixtures and fittings (known as *f and f*) include such things as carpeting, light fixtures, towel rails, and cupboards that are not built in. You may be charged a separate price for *f and f* when you buy a house; otherwise they are likely to be removed. Use their inclusion as a negotiating point. F and f can also be a euphemistic phrase for the technically illegal keymoney payment on unfurnished rental property, now thankfully quite rare.

Freehold property (see **Leasehold**).

The **garden** means the total property surrounding the house, in which there may be a *kitchen garden,* the plot where your vegetables grow.

The **garden flat** is nestled in that part of the house at least partly below ground, called the *lower ground floor* or, in the case of an apartment building, the *garden level.*

The **ground floor** in England is our first floor and, to add to the confusion, the *first floor* in England is our second. So, house hunters should remember that the first floor bedrooms are upstairs.

A **heated towel rail** in the bathroom is such a luxury — but not if it is the only source of heat in the room!

An **inglenook fireplace** is large enough to sit or stand upright in.

The term **lagged hot water cylinder with immersion heater** is a triple puzzle. The *lagging* is the padded coat your water heater wears for insulation. The *cylinder* is the hot water tank where water is stored. (The capacity should be a minimum of seven gallons for each person in the family.) The *immersion heater* takes over the task of heating the water when the furnace is not in use. It is electrically controlled and thus an expensive and inefficient way to heat water; use it only as a back-up system.

The **larder cupboard** is the pantry and is likely to be unheated, since it was used as cool storage in the days before the widespread use of refrigeration.

Leaded lights are windows with leaded panes.

When you buy a **leasehold property** (usually a city flat or maisonette, and sometimes a town house) you have bought a lease, as contradictory as that sounds. The longer the lease, the more expensive and valuable the property, and the better the investment, because this lease can, in turn, be resold by you when you leave. When the lease terminates, it reverts to the owner of the building (in the case of a flat) or the owner of the land (in the case of a house). Therefore, a leasehold property must be considered a depreciating asset, particularly in the last years of the lease. When you buy a **freehold property**, all of it is yours forever — including the land!

The **loft** is the closest thing you will have to an attic. Enter it through that mysterious trap door in the ceiling of the upstairs landing. The loft houses the storage tank and offers dry and sometimes roomy storage for the items you can wrestle through the opening.

Maisonette is the term for a duplex apartment, one that takes up more than one floor.

A **mews house** is a very charming type of row house, converted from old stables or servants' lodgings.

If your sink, washbasin, or tub has two knobs, one hot and one cold, but one single faucet out of which the water comes, you are fortunate enough to have **mixer taps.**

Your landlord is an **owner-occupier** when the house you are renting from him is his main or only residence in the U.K. This means that he can move back into his house when the lease is up, whether or not you are ready to leave.

Rates are a form of tax paid to the local government, similar to a property tax; the amount is based on the *rateable value* of your house; if you rent, it is paid by the owner of the property.

Reception rooms are, theoretically anyway, those rooms in which you can receive guests, and include the living room *(sitting room, drawing room,* or *lounge),* dining room, study, and family room. Excluded are the kitchen, the laundry room, and, of course, bedrooms.

A **self-contained annex** *(granny suite)* consists of three rooms, usually a living room/bedroom combination with a kitchenette and bathroom, the ideal guest quarters.

A **serving hatch** saves steps by allowing you to pass food from the kitchen to the dining room through this handy opening.

A **stable door**, also known as a Dutch door, opens separately in two sections, top and bottom. It can be found in some country kitchens and, of course, most stables!

The **suite** in the bathroom refers to anything porcelain — the toilet *(w.c.),* the tub, the basin, and, in some cases, the bidet. The *suite* in the living room includes the sofa and comfortable chairs.

A **telephone point,** also called a G.P.O. point, means a telephone outlet or jack, but not necessarily the telephone itself.

Houses in a row, all cozily sharing their side walls with their neighbors, are called **terraced houses** or, particularly if more modern, town houses.

The **vendor** is the one selling his property to you, and the lessor is renting his property to you (the lessee).

Woodblock flooring means a parquet floor.

HOW TO RENT A HOUSE

At some stage, you must decide whether to rent or buy, a decision that depends on several factors, many of which, like company policy, you probably have no control over. There is no doubt that buying is the riskier alternative, with these factors to consider: the mortgage rate; the exchange rate of your currency against the pound now and (prophetically) in the future when you'll be selling; the economic climate in Britain and its general trend; the geographic area in which you can afford to buy and its desirability (including proximity to London); the amount of rebuilding and refurbishing needed; and the flexibility you have about the timing of your move away from England.

Renting, while safer, is less attractive if you plan to stay in England for a longer period, because there is no assurance that you won't have to move out when the owners return. Try to get a feeling about this (called *security of tenure*) when you negotiate with your landlord; there is, however, no way of legally or morally pinning him down if he is a genuine *owner-occupier*.

Finding a House to Rent

Finding a house to rent *(lease)* is an exercise in flexibility and compromise, from the very first property you view to the very last negotiations on the one you want, so keep your sense of humor.

Although a rental house is yours as soon as you sign one fairly straightforward contract, there is much you can do before signing this tenancy agreement to prevent misunderstandings. Most houses are rented in a furnished state, partly because the owners are under the mistaken impression that legally this will make it easier for them to get you to leave when they want to move back in, and partly because they need a place to keep their furniture. Because most houses are family residences and were not originally furnished as rentals, you are confronted with the owners' taste (flowers, flowers everywhere) and their personal priorities.

Can you live with the rose-patterned carpet in the living room? Are the appliances adequate? If not, will the owner replace them? If he won't, are the water hook-ups and space adequate for yours? Will he remove the furniture you don't want or provide a place (other than the damp garage) for you to store it? Will he add any pieces you need?

It would be naive on your part to think you could move into someone else's house without having to spend some money yourself to make it comfortable. The object is to have the landlord pay for the major improvements (new carpeting, appliances, having rooms painted) while you take care of the minor ones (new curtains in the kitchen and additional bedroom cupboards). Try to split with the landlord the cost of major improvements, such as a burglar alarm system, with the idea of selling your half to the new tenants when you leave. Negotiate these points through the realtor before signing the lease, even though such details do not appear in the lease itself. Before you move in, while the house is vacant, an extensive inventory will be taken — a modest 40-page list of all the furnishings, right down to the last kitchen knife, and, more important, the condition of everything, including the crack in the wall and the spot on the carpet. Take plenty of time in the hassle of moving to go over this list, item by item, before signing it. When you leave, the inventory will be checked and you will be charged heavily for damage. The inventory discussion can leave a bad taste in your mouth. Be careful and be prepared. Part of your defense will be the cost of the improvements you have made, so keep the bills. Those small amounts can add up.

The Rental Contract *(Lease)*

When you have finally wrestled your way to contract time, bear the following in mind:

The chances are that your new landlord would like your breadwinner's company to sign this lease (**company let**). Although this makes you the tenant but not the lessee, it is not at all contradictory or unusual and means simply that the manager of the company has to sign the lease.

The **rent** may be expressed in weekly or monthly amounts, but in either case it is payable by the month (p.c.m. means per calendar month), or by the quarter. To convert a weekly rent to a monthly rent, multiply rent by 52 (weeks in a year) and divide by 12 (months in a year). Logical! One month's or one quarter's rent is due upon signing the contract.

Also due upon signing the lease is a **deposit** against breakage and damages (quaintly called *dilapidations deposit*). Legally it may be no more than one-sixth of the annual rent; in practice it is usually one month's rent. This may not be used as payment of the last month's rent.

The **term** of the lease is usually 364 days (one year minus one day) to be renewed each year, when you can also expect a rent increase, as high as 10%.

Pets are probably not allowed, but try to persuade your landlord to insert a clause allowing pets if you agree to pay for any damage and to clean any items soiled.

The **maintenance costs** on the property will be split between you and the landlord. You, the tenant, probably pay for telephone, electricity, gas or oil bills, the chimney sweep, and carpet and curtain cleaning; the owner probably pays the rates (a yearly charge similar to property tax), water, insurance, gardener, and (best of all!) major repairs to the house and appliances.

Actually, this cost sharing of maintenance is a gray area and calls for delicate diplomacy. Adopt an attitude that says, "We like your house and will take care of it for you just as if it were ours." You will be rewarded for this saintly approach by a good working relationship with your landlord.

An **escape clause** (also called a *business release clause* or *diplomatic clause*) allows both parties to get out of the contract, usually after six months have elapsed, and on 60 days' notice from the date of rent payment. In essence, it allows the tenant to avoid paying the full term if transferred and the owner/occupier to move back into his house if he is transferred back to England.

HOW TO BUY A HOUSE

The transactions for buying a house are intricate and lengthy (at least two months). Many a Mouse has gotten lost in this maze, so wend your way cautiously.

First, express your serious interest to your estate agent (not the seller) **by making an offer "subject to contract,"** an escape clause that means that you can withdraw if you have trouble with financing, or that the price can be changed if the survey reveals anything unpleasant. You may be asked to pay a **holding deposit** (token amount) to the estate agent or the vendor's solicitor. This is to show your good faith, but it is not binding and is returnable should your purchase not proceed for any reason.

At this stage either party can renege, and it is not uncommon. Don't make the mistake of thinking that because you have made an offer and the seller has accepted it, the end of the maze is in sight. This is not true, and you should keep all your options open by continuing to look at other properties, because the vendor, keeping his options open too, will continue to show his house.

ठ **Inform your solicitor**, who will set the process in motion by making various investigations and by drawing up the **draft contract,** a standard printed form which he submits to the vendor's solicitor.

ठ **Have a professional surveyor examine the property**, as it would be extremely unwise to rely solely on your own judgement. Besides reporting on the present state of the house and grounds, he can give information on any alterations you might like to carry out. The best way to find a reliable surveyor is through personal recommendation, but since you are short of those personal contacts at this point, get in touch with one of the following professional groups, which can give you the names of surveyors working in your area.

Incorporated Association of Architects and Surveyors
Jubilee House
Billing Brook Road, Weston Favell
Northampton
tel. Northampton (0604) 404121

Incorporated Society of Valuers and Auctioneers
3 Cadogan Street
London SW1
tel. 01-235 2282

Royal Institution of Chartered Surveyors
12 Great George Street
London SW1
tel. 01-222 7000

Talk frankly with your surveyor, if you get the opportunity. Think of it: this is the first professional you have met who is in your service and has your interests at heart. For this reason, do not rely on the report of the surveyor hired by the bank giving you the mortgage.

ॐ The **exchange of contracts** takes place after the surveyor's report has been completed and accepted, the draft contract has been agreed upon by both parties, and your financing has been arranged. You have to pay a deposit, usually 10% of the purchase price, to the vendor's solicitor, which will be refunded to you only if the vendor causes the sale to fall through.

From the moment of finding your dream house until now you have been extremely vulnerable, open to a particularly nasty, but perfectly legal, situation known as *gazumping*. In gazumping, the vendor accepts a higher offer, even though he has already accepted your offer, and even though you have agreed to pay the asking price. Your only recourse, apart from dropping the house altogether, is to jump into the fray and raise your offer. Once you exchange contracts, neither party can change his mind and the house is as good as yours.

ॐ **Conveyance** transfers ownership of the property to you. This document outlines in legal jargon the status of the vendor and the purchaser, the property, the price, and the date on which the transfer occurs.

ॐ **Completion** takes place when you have received the conveyance and paid the balance of the purchase price. (The vendor pays the estate agent his fee.) The house, its joys and its frustrations are now yours and, best of all, you can stop house hunting.

HOME IMPROVEMENT

If the house you just bought does not need any remodelling, you belong to a small but fortunate minority. To avoid more than your inevitable share of frustrations, contact the following organizations before you start to rebuild.

The **National Home Improvement Council** is an umbrella organization for the main professions concerned with rebuilding — builders, surveyors, architects, and manufacturers. They can tell you how to find a professional and advise you on grants available and on financing. Their publication, *Home Improvement Directory,* lists reliable specialists nationwide. It can be consulted at your local library or CAB (Citizens Advice Bureau).

National Home Improvement Council
26 Store Street
London WC1
tel. 01-636 2562

The **Royal Institute of British Architects** will send you a free leaflet listing the services its members offer, and its Clients Advisory Service can tell you how to find a local architect who specializes in the type of work you're having done.

Royal Institute of British Architects
66 Portland Place
London W1
tel. 01-580 5533

CHAPTER 2

Education for All Ages

EDUCATION FOR CHILDREN

The range of schools in England is as rich and varied as the choice of desserts on the dessert trolley. But there, unfortunately, the comparison ends. Choosing a school is a more serious matter, and you need to make an informed decision. Be sure you understand the British school system when you consider the options.

The British School System

There are three types of schooling: **state schools** (also called maintained schools); **private schools** (also called independent, fee-paying, or public schools); and **foreign schools** (including American and International schools).

State schools. Mandatory education begins at age 5, at the beginning of the school term that starts after the child's fifth birthday, at any point in the year. Mandatory education ends at age 16, but education often goes on, particularly for college-preparatory students, for two or three more years.

Although there are plenty of nursery schools and play groups, school starts officially with **primary school** (ages 5 to 11 or 12), which is sometimes divided into **infant school** (ages 5 to 7) and **junior school** (ages 7 to 11). **Secondary schools** include a few **comprehensive schools**, which accept all children and provide a wide range of education for local children; **grammar schools**, which provide a stiff academic program but require an entrance exam; and **secondary modern schools**, which are geared to students who will be leaving at age 16.

This picture is further confused by a recent trend to add a middle stage, making a three-tiered system: **first, middle, and upper schools**. The middle school (ages about 8 to 12) is meant to be a transition between the relaxed first schools and the formal teaching of the upper schools.

For more information on the British school system, ask for the following booklets:

Department of Education and Science
Elizabeth House
York Road
London SE1
tel. 01-928 9222
title: *The Educational System of England and Wales*

British Council
British Embassy, Cultural Department
Washington, D.C.
tel. (202) 462-1340, ext. 2337
title: *British Education*

The British-American Educational Foundation
426 East 89th Street
New York, N.Y. 10028
tel. (212) 772-3890
title: *About School in England*

There is no British equivalent of the American high school diploma. The **GCE (General Certificate of Education)** and the **CSE (Certificate of Secondary Education)**, soon to be combined, are offered instead. The GCE is given at **Ordinary** and **Advanced** levels. **O-level** tests are taken at age 16 (in as many as ten subjects!) and **A-level** tests, in a few selected subjects, two or three years later. The usual minimum requirement for university admission is at least two passes at A-level.

Independent schools. There are about 3,000 independent schools funded solely by fees and endowments. They are attended by

550,000 pupils, or about 6% of the school-going population. Consider the cost of this privileged education, given here per term (multiply by three for the cost per year): preparatory day school, £300 – £950; preparatory boarding school, £650 – £1225; secondary day school, £300 – £1200; secondary boarding school, £800 – £1600.

Two main types of independent schools are **preparatory schools** (called *prep*) and **public schools**. The preparatory schools cater to boys and girls (though separately, since very few are coeducational) from 7 to 12 years, to prepare them for entrance into public schools. Public schools, contrary to their name, are not for the general public at all. They are privately funded, difficult to get into, and have long waiting lists. The confusing terminology arose in the Middle Ages, to contrast the new educational institutions (public) with the normal practice of education at home (private). These schools generally require a Common Entrance Exam, to be taken around age 14, and they concentrate on achieving good results in GCE, O-level, and A-level examinations. Independent schools have traditionally been single-sex schools, but this is slowly changing. Now even such male bastions as Eton admit girls to their upper classes *(forms)*.

Educational Advice

There are about 3,000 independent schools and many of them are boarding schools. The following agencies can supply **information on specific schools** as well as give general advice:

Gabbitas-Thring Education Trust Ltd.
6 Sackville Street
London W1
tel. 01-734 0161

ISIS (Independent Schools Information Service)
26 Caxton Street
London SW1
tel. 01-222 7353
12 Vandon Street (specifically for London and the
    Southeast Region)
London SW1
tel. 01-222 7274

The Truman & Knightley Educational Trust Ltd.
78 Notting Hill Gate
London W11
tel. 01-727 1242

For counseling and testing for **children with learning disabilities**, contact this educational trust:

Developmental Center
Napier Hall, Hide Place
Vincent Square
London SW1
tel. 01-821 5760

For **advisory and counseling services on American colleges and universities:**

American College Admissions Consultants
97 Jermyn Street
London SW1
tel. 01-930 8926

Educational Futures
43 Acacia Road
London NW8
tel. Weybridge (0932) 45955

The U.S./U.K. Educational Commission
6 Porter Street
London W1
tel. 01-486 1098 (student advisory service)
      01-486 7697 (Fulbright Commission)

For classes in small groups to **prepare for American college entrance examinations**, contact one of these two agencies:

GTAC Associates	The Studyworks
FREEPOST	17 Denbigh Close
London W5 4BR	London W11
tel. 01-993 3983	tel. 01-221 2429

In making that important decision to enter your child in the British school system, there are three basic considerations: the length of your stay in England, the age of your child, and your desire to "go British."

In general, the longer your stay, the more seriously you should consider English schooling. The **length of your stay**, together with the amount of control you have over the timing of your next move, can mean that a child has time to become truly adjusted to an English school, without having to leave at an awkward time — right before his last year, for example.

The **age of your child** is important — in general, the younger the child, the more easily he will make the adjustment into (and out of) a British school. British primary schools are felt to be among the best in the world, and a child educated in them has a head start for life.

Your feelings about "going British" are so important that they can influence the whole tenor of your stay. If you (and your child, of course) want to be more involved in British life, there is no quicker way to do this than by becoming a part of a British school. There your child will meet neighborhood friends and you can chat with other mums while sharing the school run.

How to Evaluate British Schools

Your situation and your child are unique, and you are the only one who can choose the best school for both. Keep the following **generalizations** in mind while you evaluate British schools.

In British schools, there is an early emphasis on academics; reading, writing, and maths instruction starts almost immediately, even at nursery schools before mandatory education at age 5. High value is attached to learning, and this seriousness of attitude will stand a child in good stead throughout his schooling. Importance is also attached to good behavior; politeness, manners, and respect for property are emphasized. The school environment tends to be a bit sheltered, and in these days of drug problems and runaway children, that could be regarded as an asset, particularly by City Mice.

Most criticisms of the British school system center on secondary education. Because students are preparing for O-level and A-level exams, the syllabus is quite specific and narrowly defined. (American high schools, with their system of electives, are more broadly based.) Because of these exams, there is an emphasis on exam performance. The British secondary student is more a passive participant, concentrating on the acquisition of facts, rather than a self-motivated, self-directed learner. Some English schools may not be very well equipped, particularly with regard to computers, science equipment, and sports facilities. (Don't make the common mistake of dismissing an old dilapidated building, however — some of the best schools in Britain could use a coat of paint!)

American Schools (see map in Chapter 1 on housing; all of these are coeducational unless otherwise indicated)

The American Community
    Schools (ACS)
"Heywood," Portsmouth Road
Cobham, Surrey KT11 1BL
tel. Cobham (0932) 67251

This is the address of the administration office for both campuses of ACS (one at Cobham, one at Hillingdon). Grades Nursery–12, about 800 students. The Dutch School, also at the Cobham campus, is listed below.

Hillingdon Court School
Vine Lane
Hillingdon, Middlesex
tel. Uxbridge (89) 59771

Grades Pre-K – 12, about 600 students.

The American International
    School (Southbank)
55 Eccleston Square
London SW1
tel. 01-834 4686

Grades 6 – 13, 100 students, about 25% North American. They offer the International Baccalaureate.

The American School in
    London
2-8 London Road
St. John's Wood
London NW8
tel. 01-722 0101

Grades K – 12, 1700 students

London Central High School
(U.S. Air Force School)
Daws Hill Lane
High Wycombe,
Buckinghamshire HP11 1PZ
tel. High Wycombe
(0494) 21242

Some non-military-dependent students allowed, grades K – 12. The elementary school is in Ruislip (tel. 01-845 2333).

Marymount School
George Road
Kingston upon Thames,
Surrey KT12 7PE
tel. 01-949 0571
01-435 2475 (adult ed)

Girls only, grades 7 – 12, 150 day students, 100 boarding students. Students from more than 35 countries, about 25% from North America. The International Baccalaureate is offered.

TASIS (a branch of
The American School
in Switzerland)
Coldharbour Lane
Thorpe, Surrey, TW20 8TE
tel. Chertsey (09328) 65252

Grades K – 12, 400 day students and 150 boarding students in grades 8 – 12.

The American School of
Aberdeen
Craigton Road, Cults
Aberdeen, Scotland
tel. Aberdeen (0224) 868927

Grades 7 – 12, 170 students.

The American School of
Aberdeen
Fergus, Mill Timber
Aberdeen, Scotland
tel. Aberdeen (0224) 732267

Grades K – 6, 160 students. (The headmaster can be reached at the address above.)

The American School of
Edinburgh
29 Chester Street
Edinburgh, Scotland EH3 7EN
tel. Edinburgh (031) 225 9888

Both a day school (30 students) and a boarding school (10 students), Grades 7 – 12.

Other Foreign Schools (see map in Chapter 1 on housing)

Dutch

The Dutch School c/o American Community Schools "Heywood," Portsmouth Road Cobham, Surrey KT11 1BL tel. Cobham (0932) 67251	Ages 4 – 14, 150 pupils.

French

Ecole Française 59/60 Brook Green London W6 (Hammersmith) tel. 01-602 6871	Ages 4 – 11 (primary school), 260 pupils.
Lycée Français 35 Cromwell Road London SW7 tel. 01-584 6322	Ages 4 – 18, 2,500 pupils.

German

The German School Douglas House Petersham Road Richmond, Surrey tel. 01-940 5724	Ages 5 – 18.

Greek

Holland Park Greek School Greek Embassy 2 Holland Park London W11 tel. 01-221 0093	Ages 3½ – 11.

International

Hampstead International
   School
16 Netherhall Gardens
London NW3
tel. 01-794 0018

Grades pre-K – 8, 150 pupils.

International School of London
Crowndale Road
London NW1
tel. 01-388 0459

Grades 5 – 13, 200 pupils. Students from 40 different countries, about 25% British. International Baccalaureate Degree offered.

Japanese

The Japanese School of London
Gloucester Avenue
London NW1
tel. 01-485 0700

Rikkyo School in England
Rudgewick, Horsham
Sussex RH1Z 3BE
tel. Rudgewick (040 373) 2107

Norwegian

The Norwegian School
28 Arterberry Road
London SW20 (Wimbledon)
tel. 01-947 6627

Ages 2½ – 16, 70 pupils.

Spanish

Colegio Vicente Canada De
   Portobello
317a Portobello Road
London W10
tel. 01-969 2664

Ages 4 – 19, 1000 pupils.

Swedish

The Swedish School   Ages 7 – 16, 150 pupils.
82 Lonsdale Road
London SW13 (Barnes)
tel. 01-741 1751

For a map of the main American and international schools, see Chapter 1 on housing.

EDUCATION FOR ADULTS

American Universities and Colleges

In the London area, there are almost 20 colleges and universities related in some way to American educational institutions. They range alphabetically from Antioch to Warnborough, and the range of subjects and quality is even greater. The following organization can supply you with a complete listing of American colleges and universities, their status, subjects offered, and degrees conferred:

The U.S./U.K. Educational Commission
6 Porter Street
London W1
tel. 01-486 1098

Study the list of institutions with these considerations in mind:

႙ Are they accredited to offer a complete four-year Bachelor's degree? (Some offer only two years, after which you must transfer.)

႙ Do they offer the degree I seek? (Some offer only postgraduate courses.)

႙ Do they have a parent campus in the U.S.? (If they do not, credits earned here may not be automatically transferable.)

႙ Will they accept any past college work I have completed?

႙ Can I transfer my credits earned here to another U.K. college or university?

&ex; What is their accreditation?

&ex; What percentage of the student body is non-English-speaking? (A large foreign student body can slow the pace of lectures and assignments.)

&ex; What are the tuition and fees (expressed per semester or per year)?

Courses to Take

Living abroad is an educational experience in itself, and when you see how many courses there are to take, you'll find this doubly true.

A large selection is offered by the **ILEA (Inner London Education Authority)**. The City Mouse should buy a copy of their annual magazine, *Floodlight*, as soon as it hits the newsstand in August. Just look at the choice: over 50 computer courses, 40 foreign language courses, courses on calligraphy, home repairs, typing, silversmithing, dressmaking, bridge, history, antiques, and many, many more. ILEA courses are open to all adults, whatever their previous education; the cost is nominal, thanks to heavy subsidizing.

> ILEA (Inner London Education Authority)
> The County Hall
> London SE1
> tel. 01-633 1066 (Check the London phone book for the division
>   nearest you.)

Pickings are just as abundant for the Country Mouse. She can find the nearest location of county council courses by looking under her county or Local Authority in the phone book: for example, *Surrey County Council, Further Education*. A list from them will show courses given on just about any subject in almost every town.

The **Open University** offers home-based study. You receive materials by mail which are supplemented by TV and radio broadcasts. If you wish, you can study toward a Bachelor of Arts degree, but you can also take individual courses.

The Open University
P.O. Box 48
Milton Keynes MK7 6AB
tel. Milton Keynes (0908) 74066

The **University of London** offers a thousand courses, open to any
resident over the age of 18. You may also take courses for university
credit.

University of London
Department of Extra-Mural Studies
26 Russell Square
London WC1 5DP
tel. 01-636 8000

Cooking Classes

Catercall Cookery Courses
109 Stephendale Road
London SW6
tel. 01-731 3996 (Try one of their country courses at Blackdown
    House near Haslemere, Surrey, or attend a demonstration in
    Old English Style cookery in Hampstead.)

Cordon Bleu Cookery School
114 Marylebone Lane
London W1
tel. 01-935 3503 (Everything from casual Wednesday afternoon
    demonstrations to a serious diploma course.)

Divertimenti
139-141 Fulham Road
London SW3
tel. 01-581 8065 (Visit their shops full of well-designed kitchen
    supplies at this address and at 68 Marylebone Lane.)

Leith's School of Food and Wine
36a Notting Hill Gate
London W11
tel. 01-229 0177 (Courses on wine as well as food.)

Tante Marie School of Cookery
Woodham House, Carlton Road
Woking, Surrey
tel. Woking (048 62) 4050 (Cordon Bleu Certificate courses, one-day demonstrations, and wine classes.)

Winkfield Place
Winkfield, Windsor, Berkshire SL4 4RN
tel. Winkfield Row (0344) 882904 (Cordon Bleu Certificate courses, Constance Spry flower-arranging classes.)

Arts Courses

Arts courses are offered by almost all of the museums and galleries. Call them to get on their free mailing lists. Two auction houses offer interesting courses:

Christie's
63 Old Brompton Road
London SW7
tel. 01-581 3933 (Take their Fine Arts Courses either full-time or part-time for three terms, or their shorter courses and evening lectures. All of these require serious commitment on your part.)

Sotheby Parke Bernet & Co.
34-35 New Bond Street
London W2
tel. 01-262 5462 (Mainly courses in the decorative arts; acceptance after application and an interview. They also offer a Collectors' Week, and you can enroll for just one of the days.)

CHAPTER 3

Packing, Planning and Paperwork

IMPORTANT PAPERS

Work Permit

Unless you are a citizen of a Common Market country, you need a **work permit** to work in Great Britain. Your employer will apply for one on your behalf while you are still outside England. (A spouse may also work under this same permit.) The permit is valid for presentation to British Immigration at your port of arrival within four months of issue and is usually valid for 12 months of employment. Although you won't be directly involved, you may require further information:

> Department of Employment, Foreign Labour Section
> Caxton House
> Tothill Street
> London SW1
> tel. 01-213 3000

British Import License for Pets

Pets cannot be brought into Great Britain as part of your belongings unless you have applied for and been issued a British Import Licence. And that is only the beginning of a sad tale (tail?). England is virtually rabies-free, and to keep it that way all incoming pets must be quarantined in a government-approved kennel for six months immediately upon arrival.

🐾 To obtain an **import license**, you (or the kennel/carrying agent) must take the following steps:

🐾 Reserve accommodation in one of the approved kennels. Book at least eight weeks in advance. Choose a convenient location, because you will want to visit Pet often during those interminable six months.

🐾 Get the services of an authorized carrying agent. (This may be the kennel owner.) He will pick up Pet at the airport once he has received the import license and will take him to the kennel. There Poor Pet will receive a rabies inoculation, regardless of the date of his last shot.

🐾 Complete Form IDI and send it to the Ministry when you have learned that your kennel and carrying agent have been arranged. To obtain this form, a list of approved kennels and carrying agents, and more information, contact the Ministry of Agriculture:

Ministry of Agriculture, Fisheries and Food, Rabies Branch
Hook Rise South
Surbiton, Surrey KT6 7NF
tel. 01-337 6611

Alien Registration

As a foreign resident, you must register with the police within seven days of your arrival. Report personally and take your passport, work permit, and two passport pictures. You will receive a Green Card, or a stamp in your passport (which must be restamped in each new passport), proof of your registration. Take it with you when traveling abroad for easier re-entry into England. Be sure to notify the police of any address changes.

For the **City Mouse:**

Alien Registration Office
10 Lambs Conduit Street
London WC1
tel. 01-725 2451

The **Country Mouse** should register at the nearest police station, listed in the telephone directory under *Police*.

To extend your stay, write to the Home Office or go in person:

Home Office
Lunar House
40 Wellesley Road
Croydon, Surrey CR9 2BY
tel. 01-686 0688 (immigration Department Inquiries)
       01-681 3421 (Nationality Department Inquiries)

Drivers License

You need a British drivers license to drive in England, unless you are a tourist. If you are a citizen of a Common Market country, you can obtain this without a driving test. All other foreign residents, however, must pass a two-part test (both practice and theory) within a year. (For further information, see Chapter 9 on transportation.)

HOW TO DECIDE WHAT TO PACK

When you are in the midst of deciding which belongings to take with you and which to leave behind, keep this in mind: it would be difficult to think of anything you can't get in England, especially in London. The following discussion, then, is meant to save you time, money, and aggravation in those first difficult months of settling in, but it is by no means necessary for you to take the items mentioned.

⚘ **Electrical appliances.** For a detailed discussion of the problem, see Chapter 4 on electricity.

⚘ **Clothing**. The English weather has received a lot of bad press through the years, but unless your last base was a tropical island, the temperate climate here will come as a pleasant surprise. The temperature rarely drops below freezing, so you can forget about lost mittens, snow suits, and other frustrations of a severe winter. In summer you will need sweaters for cool days and evenings, and a stylish raincoat will serve you well all year through. But, no matter how pleasurable you find the English climate, avoid praising it. Complaints about the weather are a perfect conversation opener and approval of it almost taboo. You will find yourself particularly prone to positive remarks in spring, when crocuses appear as early as February and baby lambs soon after.

The following clothing articles and sizes are difficult to get: men's dress shirts, particularly with extra-long sleeves (shirts in England are sold only according to collar size, in one standard sleeve length); women's shoes in narrow widths and small sizes; women's clothes in small sizes (8 and under); teenage clothes (particularly for girls 12 – 16 years).

 Dictionary of your own language (remember, American and English usage and spelling do differ somewhat and so do the dictionaries).

 Equipment for games, sports, and celebrations of your country, such as a basketball hoop to hang in the driveway (a great attraction for neighborhood children); Halloween costumes; baseball bats and gloves; Easter egg dye; footballs; Santa Claus costume.

 Eyeglasses, contact lenses, and related prescriptions.

 Kitchen necessities such as measuring cups and spoons, cake and pie pans. (See Chapter 8 on food for a further discussion and a list of substitute ingredients.)

 Linens. Unless you are interested in formal table linens that need special care and ironing, such as the beautiful Irish linens, take along some of your own, particularly casual placemats and easy-care napkins. (Or, learn to set an English table by using Melamine placemats.) Good bathroom linens, such as towels and washable bathroom rugs, are hard to find, and the thick luxurious ones usually turn out to be imported from America so they're doubly expensive. For all linens, try the "practical shoppers' paradise" — Oxford Street between Regent Street and Marble Arch, with its abundance of department stores: John Lewis, D.H. Evans, Selfridges, Marks & Spencers, British Home Stores, and Debenhams. For bedding, consider bringing your mattress covers, permanent-press sheets, and washable blankets. You can use your electric blanket on a transformer, or you can buy a puffy comforter (*duvet,* say DOOvay). A lovely, comforting way to sleep! Keep in mind the different bed sizes, shown in the chart.

American bed sizes in inches	English bed sizes in inches and centimeters
	36″ × 75″/90cm × 190cm
single: 38″ × 75″	39″ × 78″/100cm × 200cm
double: 53″ × 75″	54″ × 75″/135cm × 190cm
queen 60″ × 80″	60″ × 78″/150cm × 200cm
king 76″ × 80″	70″ × 78″/180cm × 200cm

Medicines, certainly those on prescription, but also those to which you are addicted — figuratively speaking, of course — such as your favorite cold remedy or vitamin tablets.

HOW TO GET THROUGH CUSTOMS

Your **belongings** (such as household effects and clothing) may be brought in free of duty as long as you have owned and used them for at least 6 months prior to your move. Your goods may precede you by 6 months and may follow you by 12 months, in which case your mover or shipping agent must present a customs declaration (Form C3) and a detailed packing list at the border.

For forms and notices inquire at any Customs and Excise Office, or write to them:

HM Customs and Excise Department
King's Beam House
Mark Lane
London EC3
tel. 01-626 1515

There are some **prohibited goods**, most of them quite logical: controlled drugs (such as heroin, cocaine, cannabis); counterfeit money; firearms; obscene books and tapes; meat and poultry; plants and vegetables; animals and birds (both alive and stuffed).

Restricted goods, including wine, spirits, and tobacco, may be imported in limited amounts.

The fate in store for Poor Pet is described fully at the beginning of this chapter under Important Papers, but to add insult to injury, you will be charged a tax on the purchase price or replacement value of Pet. Fill out Form C3 for this; or the carrier can do it along with the other paperwork.

Your **car** may be brought in duty-free if you have owned it for more than 6 months. Bring with you proof of use outside England, such as registration papers and insurance policy. You will probably decide not to import your car with the steering wheel on the "wrong side." Consider, however, a **tax-free car** from these people, who can give you more information:

Shipside Tax Free World on Wheels B.V.
Shipside Building
P.O. Box 7568
1118 ZH Schiphol Airport
The Netherlands
tel. (020) 15 28 33

Shipside Car Delivery Inc.
576 Fifth Avenue, 7th floor
New York, N.Y. 10036
tel. (202) 869 4484
(800) 223 0919

For estimate of **duty and tax** on motor vehicles:

HM Customs and Excise, Valuation Division
Vintry House
Queen Street Place
London EC4
tel. 01-626 1515

For information on car **insurance**, licenses, British registration numbers, and the use of foreign plates:

Driver and Vehicle Licensing Centre (DVLC)
Longview Road
Swansea SA6 7JL
tel. Swansea (0792) 72134

CHAPTER 4

Electricity and Appliances

ELECTRICAL APPLIANCES

When moving to England, the question concerning which U.S. electrical appliances to take with you is a complicated one. Electric current in England is 240 volts, 50Hz, while U.S. current is 110 volts, 60Hz, and this fact will give you a lot of headaches — the larger appliances (washer, dryer, and refrigerator) producing the larger headaches. There are four possible solutions to this:

⚬ **Solution 1: You can take your 110-volt appliances with you and use them with transformers to step up the voltage.** The disadvantages are that spare parts may be time-consuming to obtain; the appliances may be too big for your English kitchen or laundry area; and using transformers for a long time may cause the appliances to wear out much sooner.

Transformers should correspond approximately in size (wattage) with the appliance they are connected to, as shown in the chart.

Transformer size	Appliances (check the wattage on *your* appliance)
100 watts	electric blanket, small radio and tape recorder, record player, can opener
250 watts	radio, stereo, small food mixer, blender
500 watts	refrigerator, large mixer, power drill

750 watts	freezer, heated trolley, percolator
1000 watts	coffee maker, vacuum cleaner, food processor, toaster, hair dryer
2000 watts	hot plate, iron
3000 watts	heater, dishwasher, electric kettle, clothes dryer, washing machine

Small electrical appliances such as a blender, mixer, food processor, coffee pot, toaster, and waffle iron can all be used on transformers. Don't, however, underestimate the large "nuisance factor" with transformers.

❧ Solution 2: You can buy American-brand appliances wired for European current, that is, 220 or 240 volt, 50 Hz, before you move. Space for the larger appliances in your English house may be limited, so measure carefully. Order from these companies:

Thor Export Sales Co., Inc
130 Madison Avenue
New York, N.Y. 10016
tel. (212) 679-0077

Algert Appliance Co., Inc
1801 W 8th St.
Los Angeles, CA 90057
tel. (213) 483-2335

❧ Solution 3: You can buy European appliances in England. Almost all washing machines are front-loading, which means that if your dryer is of the same make, you can stack the two — a marvellous space-saver. You can choose between models that heat their own water *(cold-fill)* and those that are hooked up to the main hot-water system *(hot-and-cold fill)*. Make sure the washing machine spins at 1000 rpm or your clothes will be so wet that the dryer will not work efficiently. Consider the top models of these brands: AEG, Miele, Zanussi, Hoover, Philips, and Bendix.

The following **wash code** appears on clothing labels and should correspond to the symbols on your washing machine programs:

Examples of application

	MACHINE	HAND WASH	
1 **95**	Very hot to boil maximum wash	Hand-hot or boil	
		Spin or wring	

White cotton and linen articles without special finishes

	MACHINE	HAND WASH	
2 **60**	Hot maximum wash	Hand-hot	
		Spin or wring	

Cotton, linen or viscose articles without special finishes where colours are fast at 60°C

	MACHINE	HAND WASH	
3 **60**	Hot medium wash	Hand-hot	
		Cold rinse. Short spin or drip-dry	

White nylon; white polyester/cotton mixtures

	MACHINE	HAND WASH	
4 **50**	Hand-hot medium wash	Hand-hot	
		Cold rinse. Short spin or drip dry	

Coloured nylon; polyester; cotton and viscose articles with special finishes; acrylic/cotton mixtures; coloured polyester/cotton mixtures

	MACHINE	HAND WASH	
5 **40**	Warm maximum wash	Warm	
		Spin or wring	

Cotton, linen or viscose articles where colours are fast at 40°C, but not at 60°C

	MACHINE	HAND WASH	
6 **40**	Warm minimum wash	Warm	
		Cold rinse. Short spin. Do not wring	

Acrylics; acetate and triacetate, including mixtures with wool; polyester/wool blends

	MACHINE	HAND WASH	
7 **40**	Warm minimum wash	Warm Do not rub	
		Spin. Do not hand wring	

Wool, including blankets and wool mixtures with cotton or viscose; silk

	MACHINE	HAND WASH	
8 **30**	Cool minimum wash	Cool	
		Cold rinse. Short spin. Do not wring	

Silk and printed acetate fabrics with colours not fast at 40°C

	MACHINE	HAND WASH	
9 **95**	Very hot to boil minimum wash	Hand-hot or boil	
		Drip-dry	

Cotton articles with special finishes capable of being boiled but requiring drip drying

	HAND WASH
(hand symbol)	

Articles which must not be machine washed. Details will vary because garment manufacturers are free to put their own written instructions on this label

If laundry space is at a premium, consider one appliance that both washes and dries in the same drum (called an *integral washer/dryer*). Its drawback is that you can't dry your full washer load at one time.

The largest **refrigerators** have a capacity of about 10 cu. ft. or 285 liters. Try the larger models of Hoover and Tricity, two brand names mentioned by *WHICH?*, a monthly magazine published by the Consumers' Association.

Read up on other appliances in *WHICH?*, available at your local library. For consumer advice and information, become a member:

WHICH? Subscription Department
Consumers' Association
FREEPOST, Hertford SG13 8BR
tel. Hertford (0992) 59031

If you need help with consumer problems, contact your nearest Citizens' Advice Bureau (CAB) for free advice. You can find the address of the nearest office at your local library.

Start your own market research for appliances at John Lewis, a large department store in Oxford Street, London, since they still claim to have the lowest prices in town. Harrods carries American models if you're willing to pay their prices. The following chains offer discount prices on household appliances but may not have a full range displayed. Be sure to ask if there is an additional charge for delivery. Their branches are listed in the phone book: Comet Discount Warehouse, Temp Electrical Stores, Electrical Discount Stores, Argos (catalogue and showroom service), and Currys.

You can be sure of the safety of your new electrical appliances if you see this symbol:

🍄 **Solution 4: You can buy second-hand American appliances** from others who are moving away from England. Although the timing on this is tricky, read the classified ads connected with the American Women's Clubs, particularly in the spring, during the mass exodus of expatriates. Don't forget to add the transport costs to the cost of the appliances.

Lamps are easy to convert. Simply change the plug to fit an English wall socket and put in a 240-volt bulb. Screw-in bulbs are becoming more readily available, but since English lamps normally take a bulb with a clip-in *(bayonet cap)* fitting, they are not available in all stores. Rather than change the fitting, seek out a supplier of appropriate bulbs, either a large department store or a local electricity shop.
For a large selection of reproduction Victorian lamps:

Christopher Wray
600 King's Road
London SW6
tel. (01) 736 8008

Your **stereo amplifier, tuner/receiver** will work on a transformer. **Tape decks** and **record players** can normally be converted from 60Hz to 50Hz operation, generally a simple procedure which is reversible. Check with a stereo shop to be sure that your particular model is convertible. (A few models will run on either 50 or 60Hz.) Your **television set, video recorder,** and **electric clock** cannot be adapted; your **sewing machine, electric typewriter,** and **vacuum cleaner** can be used with transformers, but they may work less efficiently or wear out more quickly. Ask the manufacturers (not a retailer) about your **computer** and **microwave oven.**

HOW TO WIRE A PLUG

Almost all electrical appliances and equipment that you buy in England will come without a plug attached. You are expected to attach a plug. It's an operation that seems complicated only to the uninitiated, so study the following instructions and the illustrations.

You will need a screwdriver, a wire stripper (or failing that, a sharp knife), a white plug with three gold-colored pins, and the proper fuse. Prepare the electric cord by stripping off about two inches of the outer covering. You will now see three smaller insulated cords of different colors: brown for live; blue for neutral; and green and yellow for ground *(earth)*. Older plugs will have an outdated color scheme: red (live), black (neutral), and green (ground). Then, strip the insulation off these small cords, about half an inch at the very end, right down to the fine strands of wire inside.

How to Wire a Plug

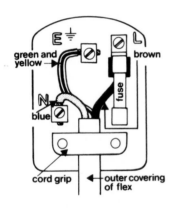

green and yellow

brown

fuse

N

blue

cord grip ← outer covering of flex

Unscrew and remove the cover of the plug. Loosen the pillar terminals slightly and one side of the clamp that will hold the wire in place. Pass the whole wire under the clamp and tighten it firmly. Twist the exposed strands of each cord together and insert each bunch of strands in the hole near the top of the appropriate terminal: blue (neutral) on the left, brown (live) on the right next to the fuse, and green and yellow (ground) to the middle terminal. Tighten each of the three screws to hold the twisted strands firmly in place.

Place a cartridge fuse in the clamps on the right. (Fuses for plugs are marked BS 1362, to distinguish them from those used in the fuse box.) Use a red, 3-amp fuse for appliances up to 720 watts (lamps, blankets, etc.) and a brown, 13-amp fuse for appliances over 720 watts (irons, heaters, large appliances) or appliances that have an initial surge of electricity when turned on (vacuum cleaners, food freezers). When in doubt, check the manufacturer's instructions.

Be careful and accurate. Electric current has a pressure of 240 volts (more than double the American voltage), reason enough to treat electricity with respect. Before you replace the cover of the plug, make sure that there are no stray whiskers of bare wire and that the wires are very tightly screwed down. Connections or screws to the wrong terminal can prove lethal.

Now screw the plug back together. What a sense of accomplishment! You deserve a pat on the back.

HOW TO REPLACE A FUSE

There are three kinds of fuses possible in the fuse box controlling the domestic electrical circuit, **circuit breakers, cartridge fuses,** and **rewireable fuses.** Unfortunately, the most complicated system is also the most common.

Circuit Breakers

The simplest system contains the new miniature **circuit breakers.** When a fuse is overloaded, it automatically switches itself off. You can tell at a glance which circuit breaker has tripped because the switch is in the *off* position. To restore electricity, simply press the switch or button.

Cartridge Fuses

A few fuse boxes have **cartridge fuses**; it is easy to replace these, but difficult to find the one to replace. To find the guilty fuse, turn off the main switch and remove the most likely suspect. Unscrew the two parts of the fuse carrier and remove the cartridge fuse. Use a metal flashlight to check the fuse like this: switch on the flashlight. Then unscrew the bottom cap and place the suspect fuse so that one end touches the metal base of the battery and the other touches the metal of the flashlight case. If the flashlight lights, then the fuse is still intact, and you have to move on to the next one. If you don't have a metal flashlight, use the trial-and-error approach to find the faulty fuse. Systematically replace each fuse with another

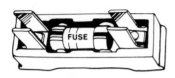

Cartridge Fuse

one, replace the carrier, and turn on the main switch. Repeat this until you have found the blown fuse. Don't forget to turn off the main switch before you remove each fuse.

When you have found the culprit, simply replace the blown fuse with a new cartridge. Make sure that it is marked BS 1361, to distinguish it from the plug cartridge fuses, and that it is the correct amperage for the circuit it protects. The fuse carriers themselves are color-coded; 5A is white (for lighting); 15A is blue; 20A is yellow (for hot water heaters); 30A is red; and 45A is green (for stoves).

Rewireable Fuses

Most fuse boxes contain rewireable fuses; when a fuse blows you must replace the wire inside the fuse carrier. It is easy to tell which fuse to replace, because the wire will be broken and there may even be scorch marks around it. Turn off the main switch. Take out the fuse carrier, remove the broken fuse wire, and replace it with the correct size of copper wire from the card of wire that you keep next to the fuse box. The fuse carriers themselves may be color-coded: 5 amp (white), 15 amp (blue), and 30 amp (red).

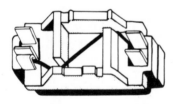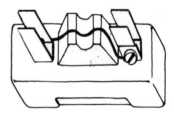

Rewireable Fuses

Cut off a short piece of wire, twist it clockwise around one of the screws, and tighten the screw; twist the other end of the wire around the other screw in a counterclockwise direction and tighten, being careful not to stretch the wire. Cut off any spare wire, and replace the fuse carrier.

If a fuse continues to blow, call an approved electrical contractor who is listed with the National Inspection Council for Electrical Installation Contracting (NICEIC).

INFORMATION ON ELECTRICITY

For more information on electrical questions, contact the following remarkable organization. They offer classes, film strips, an informative booklet called *Electricity for Everyday Living,* and even linen tea towels with graphic designs of plugs and fuses. Their diversity is electrifying!

Electrical Association for Women
25 Foubert's Place
London W1
tel. 01-437 5212

YOUR ELECTRICITY BILL

Your quarterly electricity bill will consist of a basic charge, either a fixed amount or a number of higher-priced units, and a charge for the number of units used, taken from the two meter readings, also stated on the bill. (The letter A means that there has not been a reading and that the number of units used has been assessed or estimated.) You can decrease your electricity bill by applying for a special day/night tariff, known as the Economy 7 or the White Meter Tariff, which will give you cheap electricity during the night.

Although you can pay for your electricity quarterly, it is easier to have your Electricity Board make a monthly estimate of your bill. Then you should complete their **standing order form.** The bills will be paid directly from your bank account or National Giro Account, without your direct intervention. You will continue to receive quarterly statements from the Electricity Board, however.

THE ELECTRICITY BOARD

Your Electricity Board (in southeast England, known as SEEboard) brings you much more than just electric current. Their shops, found in almost every town, offer an extensive range of appliances, all in stock, and all carrying a 12-month guarantee. They also service and maintain appliances bought elsewhere and carry a large supply of parts. They can modernize your existing electrical installation or install new wiring.

Look in your regular telephone directory (not the Yellow Pages) under *electricity* to find a whole page of information: your district office, repairs and service, emergency service, energy advice, and some shops.

CHAPTER 5

How To Survive in Style:
Culture Shock

As the title of this book implies, mere survival in England is not
enough. We want to start enjoying our new life as soon as possible,
to concentrate on the rewards of living in a foreign culture, and to
minimize the frustrations of adjusting to that culture. In short, our
goal is to survive in style.

The biggest hindrance to surviving in style is a condition known
as **culture shock.** You can often diagnose and cure your own case of
culture shock, as long as you keep in mind its **definition,** its
causes, its **symptoms,** and its **treatment.**

Definition. Culture shock can be defined as a sense of
disorientation and the resulting anxiety and stress when we are
transplanted from one culture to another.

Causes. The causes are deep-rooted but stem from the fact that
we have become strangers in a strange land. All through our lives,
we have behaved according to familiar cues from our surroundings
— the general behavior around us, the words people use, their facial
expressions and body language, the norms of the groups we identify
with. Now most of these guides and cues for our own behavior have
fallen away, to be replaced by unreadable ones: Should I shake
hands with him? Do I answer *yes* or *no* when she begins her
sentences with, *Would you mind terribly if I . . .?* If she's friendly,
why isn't she smiling? Because clues like these are new and their
messages unfamiliar, we end up feeling insecure and even resentful
that we have to put so much effort into daily things that were once
completely automatic.

To make matters worse, we also experience a clash between our
beliefs and our actions. In trying to survive in a new culture and in

trying to adjust to new cues, we change the way we do things, we act in ways that are contrary to our long-held habits. For example, we learn to speak more softly, we learn new rules of the road, we learn shop closing hours, and we even learn new pronunciations for familiar words. We adopt this new behavior in order to survive, but somehow we still believe that the old way of doing things is the right way. The way we did things "at home" makes more sense than the way they're done in England. We are thrown into conflict — when we try to adapt, our actions don't coincide with our beliefs.

Symptoms. What are the symptoms of culture shock? There seem to be inevitable stages that we all go through in cultural adjustment. Here is a brief description of the **four general stages:**

First: If, when talking about your impending move, your stomach twists in excitement and anticipation, you are experiencing the first symptoms of culture shock, generally pleasant symptoms that continue through your move and well into the first months of your stay in England. This **first stage** manifests itself in anticipation and exhilaration at your good fortune in being abroad, and some people never progress beyond this state of mild euphoria. Their whole stay in England consists of behaving like permanent tourists: traveling to new and wonderful places, forming friendships exclusively with other expatriates, and maintaining their old lifestyle. Like the honeymoon period (to which it is often compared) it is pleasant, but a stage you should grow out of if you want to truly survive in style.

Second: Don't get mired down in the **second stage** of culture shock, marked by discouragement, doubt about your own capabilities, apathy, and a generally negative attitude toward England. Your conversations during this stage tend to concentrate on the things you can't buy, the things you have to do without, and all the things the English do "wrong" (which means "differently"). Complaints about everything, from repairmen who arrive late to discourteous drivers, lie close below the surface of every conversation.

Third: With perseverance, you will progress to the **third stage** before the end of the first year. You are now learning the cues of English culture and you hardly ever experience that old sense of disorientation. You have met English neighbors and have had them to dinner; you have taken a good course in English history; you even discover British vocabulary and pronunciation creeping into your speech. You are becoming immersed in the English way of life, rather than standing on the outside, critically looking in.

Fourth: The **fourth, final, and most pleasant stage** of cultural adjustment is marked by full participation in the English way of life. Now, you rarely find yourself thinking in the categories of "them" and "us."

Treatment. There are three steps in the treatment of culture shock. **First** of all, apply the old saying, "An ounce of prevention is worth a pound of cure." You can minimize cultural maladjustment by thorough preparation. Get as much information as you can about England and your assignment, both from the employer sending you and from people who have lived there.

In the **second** step of treatment, try to fend off feelings of depression by taking concrete measures to adapt; for example, familiarize yourself with your immediate surroundings. Keep your explorations local and leave the rest of London and England until later. Buy maps of your locality and trace some of the routes on foot; read local newspapers, clip addresses, file some away, and visit others. More important, familiarize yourself with your surroundings in an emotional sense. Chat with the local shopkeeper; have a cup of tea at the local coffee shop to do some subtle people-watching; become a regular reader of the notice board at your local library and join one of the activities listed there.

Acquire basic information before you need it: contact a doctor and dentist before the need arises; familiarize yourself with emergency medical procedures; plan the steps to take if your car breaks down; learn about public transportation.

Ask advice, even though you feel your foreign accent makes you conspicuous. People like giving it and you know you can certainly use it!

The **third and final step of treatment** is to establish a goal and take steps to achieve it. Have you ever wanted to study art, learn a second language, develop a green thumb, hike regularly in the countryside, collect antiques? This constructive phase is like a reward for the initial frustrating phases of cultural adjustment. You can now concentrate on style, rather than survival.

By this time you will probably have developed a workable philosophy about your stay in England. If not, try the following formula, which has proved successful for the author of this book: It's a blend of fatalism (Things have been this way for years and who am I to expect to change them?), enthusiasm (It's a wonderful country and I'm lucky to be here), and opportunism (I'm going to take advantage of this once-in-a-lifetime chance). Armed with this philosophy, you can **survive in style**!

CHAPTER 6

Medical Care

THE CHOICE: NATIONAL HEALTH OR PRIVATE CARE?

England boasts two health care systems that operate side by side, not in competition but in cooperation. The first is the remarkable **National Health Service (NHS)**, under which all residents, including expatriates, receive free or nearly free health care: doctor's appointments, inoculations, prescriptions, eyeglasses, dental care, and hospital stays. Under the second system, private health care, you or your private insurance company pays for the same services.

Since most doctors, specialists, and hospitals take both private and NHS patients, the basic difference between these two systems boils down to one word: time. If you want to see a particular specialist quickly or to have elective surgery done soon, you will have a better chance if you are a private patient. You may also get more choice as to when you go to the hospital and choice of surgeon. It is unlikely, however, that you will get better medical or surgical care.

But you don't have to choose one system above the other; instead, step across the dividing line any time you wish. For example, you may be registered with your GP as a National Health patient but consult a specialist *(consultant)* as a private patient in order to be helped more promptly; you may have routine dental work done on the National Health, but complicated dental surgery done privately. You can choose whether to enter the hospital as a private or a National Health patient, since many NHS hospitals have private beds or a private wing.

Take questions about your elegibility for NHS (or that of your foreign visitors) to your local Citizens' Advice Bureau, your local DHSS (listed under *Health and Social Security* in the phone book), or one of these main offices:

> Department of Health and Social Security (DHSS)
> Alexander Fleming House, Elephant & Castle
> London SE1
> tel. 01-407 5522

> DHSS
> Newcastle upon Tyne NE98 1YX
> tel. Tyneside (091) 2857111

For partially free medical coverage while traveling abroad, apply for an E111 from the DHSS in England before leaving. You can apply for an E111 if you meet two requirements:

⚕ You must be a national of the U.K. or another EEC country.

⚕ You must normally live in the U.K.

Since North Americans do not meet the first requirement above, coverage is questionable. Contact your local DHSS office for clarification.

Learn more about the NHS from the following book. Topics include general practitioners, child health services, medical records, maternity services, and consent to treatment.

> *A Patient's Guide to the National Health Service*
> Consumers' Association
> Castlemead, Gascoyne Way
> Hertford SG14 1LH
> tel. Hertford (0992) 59031

The main private medical insurance company is

> BUPA (British United Provident Association)
> Provident House
> Essex Street
> London WC2
> tel. 01-353 5212

YOUR DOCTOR (GP)

The whole intricate health care system rests on the shoulders of your family doctor *(general practitioner)*. He will get to know you and your family and will refer you, when necessary, to more sophisticated treatment: specialists, hospital, or laboratory testing.

In addition, your general practitioner forms a liaison with the community — the community nurse, midwives, Meals on Wheels, Home Help, etc., he may assist in finding other health care facilities, such as a dental surgeon, optician, physical therapist, etc.; and he can pass on to you information about such fringe health services as acupuncture, homeopathy, etc.

Before you need a doctor, find one and pay him a visit. If you find each other congenial, register with him. If you wish to register as a National Health patient, the doctor himself will apply for your medical card (and one for each member of the family); this may take as long as four months, but you can go to him for treatment in the meantime. The following sources will have lists of doctors in your area:

local library
Department of Health
post office
American Embassy (or your embassy)
Family Practitioner Committee
Community Health Council (under C in your phone book)

Before you register with a GP and before you decide whether to register as a National Health patient or privately, consider these factors:

the geographical area covered by the practice
the number of doctors, if a group practice
the appointments system at the doctor's office *(surgery)*
the procedure for home visits
the cost of treatment

THE SPECIALIST *(CONSULTANT)*

When you need a specialist, your GP will refer you to one, whether you are a private or a National Health patient. (Under the NHS, the choice may be his, not yours!) Your GP will continue to keep track of your progress during the course of treatment with the specialist.

Specialists generally take both private and National Health patients, and hospitalization under them can be either private or NHS (though NHS patients often face a longer waiting period for non-emergencies).

Specialists who are also surgeons display the letters FRCS (Fellow of the Royal College of Surgeons). In seeming contradiction to their high rank in the medical world, they are addressed as Mister, Mrs., or Miss, instead of Doctor.

HOSPITALS

Hospitals are divided into two categories, National Health and private; but here too the distinction is blurred, because many NHS hospitals have some private beds or even whole wings. Generally, under the NHS your bed will be in a ward, while the private patient may have a private room.

Not all hospitals have emergency room facilities *(Casualty Department)* and even those that do are not always open 24 hours a day. Locate the one nearest your house.

Emergency Services — London Hospitals (Casualty Department)

Charing Cross Hospital, W6
Middlesex Hospital, W1
Royal Free Hospital, NW3
St. Bartholomew's Hospital, EC1
St. Stephen's Hospital, SW10
St. Thomas' Hospital, SE1
University College Hospital, WC1
Westminster Hospital, SW1

Emergency Services — South of London (Casualty Department)
Ashford Hospital, Ashford

Epsom Hospital, Epsom
Frimley Park Hospital, Camberley
Heatherwood Hospital, Ascot
Kingston Hospital, Kingston-on-Thames
Royal Surrey County Hospital, Guildford
St. George's Hospital, Tooting, SW17
St. Peter's Hospital, Chertsey

Private Hospitals — London
Harley Street Clinic, W1 (AMI Hospital)
Humana Hospital Wellington, NW8
London Clinic, W1
Parkside Hospital, Wimbledon, SW19
Princess Grace, W1 (AMI Hospital)

Private Hospitals — South of London
Ashtead Hospital, Ashtead
Mount Alvernia Hospital, Guildford
Nuffield Hospital, Woking
Parkside Hospital, Wimbledon, NW8
Princess Margaret Hospital, Windsor (AMI Hospital)

MATERNITY SERVICES

If you decide to have your baby on the National Health, your prenatal *(antenatal)* and postnatal care will be provided free, either by your own GP or an obstetrician or at a hospital clinic (where you are unlikely to see the same doctor each time).

If you decide to have a private-care baby, choose your busy obstetrician well in advance and get to know the hospital where he practices (you will probably see him at his office outside the hospital). Make sure the hospital is equipped to handle neo-natal complications; be especially critical when considering private clinics.

Classes for expectant mums (and dads!) are popular. For information, inquire with this voluntary organization of mothers who give advice on childbirth, nursing, and related subjects.

The National Childbirth Trust
9 Queensborough Terrace
London W2
tel. 01-229 9319

A **midwife** will be in attendance during the birth of your baby. She is qualified and legally permitted to deliver babies, not at all a remnant of the Middle Ages as the term "midwife" might make you think. She will call in a doctor if there are complications. She will continue to visit you and Baby for 10 days.

You may deliver your baby at home on the NHS, but a nice compromise is now possible. You can have your baby at the hospital and return home again within six hours, happily accompanied by your midwife!

Take your newborn to the Well-Baby Clinic at your local medical center. There Baby will be weighed, examined, and inoculated, and you will be patted, comforted, and reassured.

FAMILY PLANNING

The Family Planning Association gives assistance in contraception, pregnancy testing, and even marital problems. Your nearest office will be listed under *Family Planning* in the phone book, or call the national office:

The Family Planning Association
27 Mortimer Street
London W1
tel. 01-636 7866 (All inquiries and national office)
tel. 01-637 1818 (Recorded advice service)

The Well-Woman clinic at your local medical center may also give free contraceptive advice and supply birth control necessities for a nominal fee. Pap smears can be done there too.

DENTAL CARE

Under the NHS, all dental checkups are free. For further treatment, such as fluoride treatments, fillings, crowns, etc., there is a scale of charges (published in a booklet called *NHS Dental Treatment,* available at the post office). But even these services are free if you are a full-time student under the age of 19, if you are expecting a baby or have had one in the last year, or if you have a low income.

You can also see a private dentist, whose practice usually consists entirely of private patients.

Fluoridated water is the exception in England. You can buy small fluoride tablets without a prescription at the drugstore *(chemist)* and give to your children up to age 12.

EYE CARE

An NHS eye test is free. Consult one of these three specialists: an **ophthalmic medical practitioner**, who is qualified to give eye tests; an **ophthalmic optician**, who can supply glasses as well as give the eye tests; a **dispensing optician**, who is mainly qualified to supply glasses on the basis of your prescription, although he may provide NHS eye-testing services. There is a basic charge for NHS lenses and frames. The private patient has more choice of frames.

TERMINOLOGY

British English	American English
casualty department	emergency room
chemist (dispensing)	drugstore or pharmacy (fills prescriptions)
consultant	specialist
GP (general practitioner)	doctor
surgery	doctor's office

ALTERNATIVE MEDICINE

For information about **alternative or holistic medicine** in general, contact this organization for the name of a volunteer in your area who can give you local information:

Institute for Complementary Medicine
21 Portland Place
London W1
tel. 01-636 9543

For a list of homeopathic doctors, hospitals, and drugstores, contact this organization:

The British Homeopathic Association
27a Devonshire Street
London W1
tel. 01-935 2163

HEALTH FARMS

Health farms are very appropriately named; these places make you feel and look healthier, with their sunlamps, heat treatments, and body massages, and, like real farms, they are situated in lovely rolling fields, in manor houses just fit for a gentleman farmer of the last century.

Champneys at Tring
Tring, Hertfordshire HP23 6HY
tel. Berkhamsted (04427) 3351

Forest Mere
Liphook, Hampshire GU30 7JQ
tel. Liphook (0429) 722051

Grayshott Hall
Grayshott, near Hindhead, Surrey
tel. Hindhead (042873) 4331

Inglewood
Kintbury, Berkshire RG15 0SL
tel. Hungerford (0488) 82022

Shrubland Hall
Coddenham, Ipswich IP6 9QH
tel. Ipswich (0473) 830404

CHAPTER 7

How To Measure It:
Charts and Tables

AMERICAN CUPS	OUNCES	IMPERIAL (PINTS)	METRIC
1/4	2	1/10	60 mL. or 0.6 dL.
1/2	4	1/5	120 mL. or 1.2 dL.
3/4	6	3/10	180 mL. or 1.8 dL.
1	8	2/5	240 mL. or 2.4 dL.
2 1 AMER. PINT	16	4/5	480 mL. or 4.8 dL.
4 1 QUART	32	1 3/5	950 mL. or 9.5 dL.

BASED ON AMERICAN MEASURES.

1. Liquid Measures for Cooking (based on American measures)

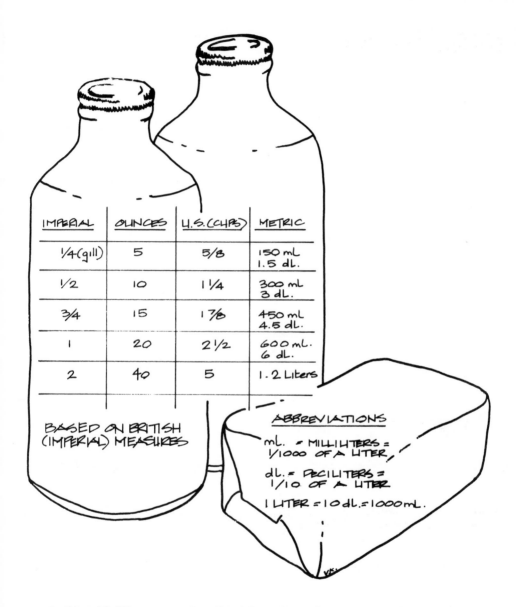

IMPERIAL	OUNCES	U.S. (CUPS)	METRIC
1/4 (gill)	5	5/8	150 mL 1.5 dL.
1/2	10	1 1/4	300 mL 3 dL.
3/4	15	1 7/8	450 mL 4.5 dL.
1	20	2 1/2	600 mL. 6 dL.
2	40	5	1.2 Liters

BASED ON BRITISH (IMPERIAL) MEASURES

ABBREVIATIONS

mL. = MILLILITERS = 1/1000 OF A LITER,

dL. = DECILITERS = 1/10 OF A LITER

1 LITER = 10 dL. = 1000 mL.

2. Liquid Measures for Cooking (based on British/Imperial measures)

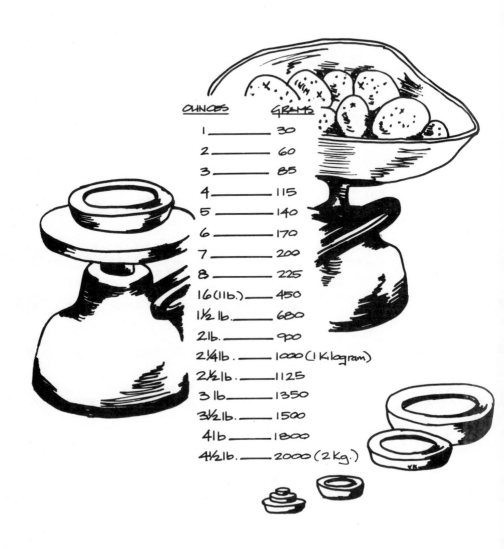

OUNCES	GRAMS
1	30
2	60
3	85
4	115
5	140
6	170
7	200
8	225
16 (1 lb.)	450
1½ lb.	680
2 lb.	900
2¼ lb.	1000 (1 Kilogram)
2½ lb.	1125
3 lb.	1350
3½ lb.	1500
4 lb.	1800
4½ lb.	2000 (2 Kg.)

3. Dry Measures for Cooking

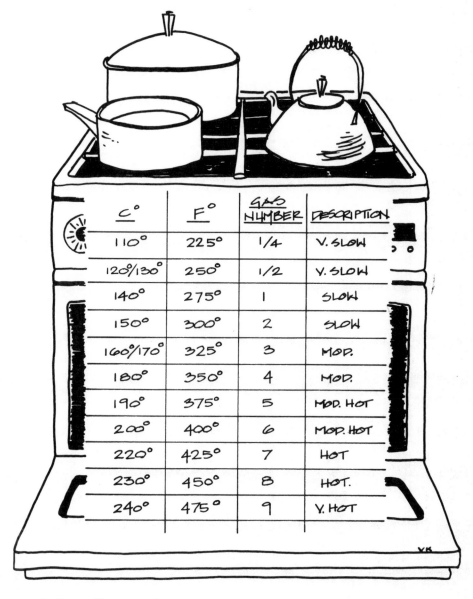

C°	F°	GAS NUMBER	DESCRIPTION
110°	225°	1/4	V. SLOW
120°/130°	250°	1/2	V. SLOW
140°	275°	1	SLOW
150°	300°	2	SLOW
160°/170°	325°	3	MOD.
180°	350°	4	MOD.
190°	375°	5	MOD. HOT
200°	400°	6	MOD. HOT
220°	425°	7	HOT
230°	450°	8	HOT.
240°	475°	9	V. HOT

4. Oven Temperatures

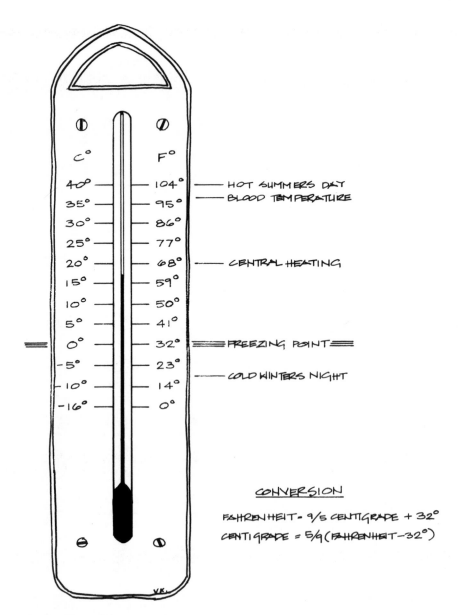

5. Outdoor Temperatures

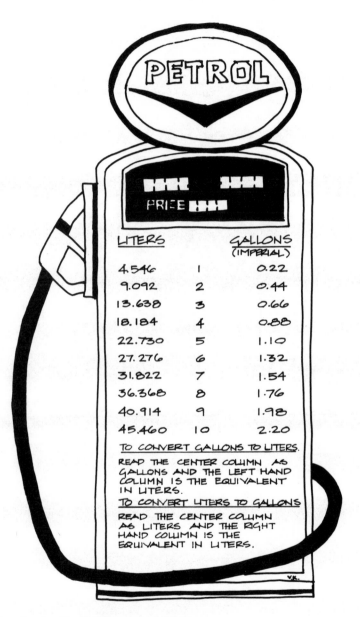

LITERS		GALLONS (IMPERIAL)
4.546	1	0.22
9.092	2	0.44
13.638	3	0.66
18.184	4	0.88
22.730	5	1.10
27.276	6	1.32
31.822	7	1.54
36.368	8	1.76
40.914	9	1.98
45.460	10	2.20

TO CONVERT GALLONS TO LITERS.

READ THE CENTER COLUMN AS GALLONS AND THE LEFT HAND COLUMN IS THE EQUIVALENT IN LITERS.

TO CONVERT LITERS TO GALLONS

READ THE CENTER COLUMN AS LITERS AND THE RIGHT HAND COLUMN IS THE EQUIVALENT IN LITERS.

6. Gas (petrol), Gallons and Liters

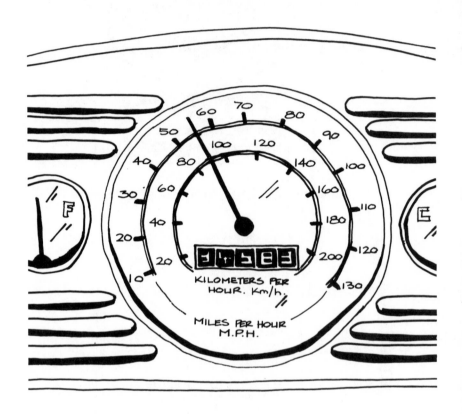

7. Speed Conversion

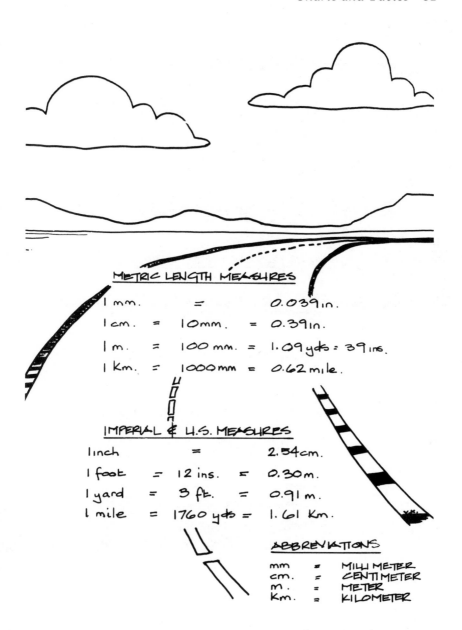

METRIC LENGTH MEASURES

1 mm.	=			0.039 in.	
1 cm.	=	10mm.	=	0.39 in.	
1 m.	=	100 mm.	=	1.09 yds	= 39 ins.
1 Km.	=	1000mm	=	0.62 mile.	

IMPERIAL & U.S. MEASURES

1 inch	=			2.54cm.
1 foot	=	12 ins.	=	0.30 m.
1 yard	=	3 ft.	=	0.91 m.
1 mile	=	1760 yds	=	1.61 Km.

ABBREVIATIONS

mm	=	MILLI METER
cm.	=	CENTI METER
m.	=	METER
Km.	=	KILOMETER

8. Length Measurements

WOMEN'S COATS, SUITS, DRESSES & BLOUSES.

BRITISH	10	12	14	16	18	20
AMERICAN	8	10	12	14	16	18
CONTINENTAL	38	40	42	44	46	48

WOMEN'S SHOES.

BRITISH	3	4	5	6	7	8	9
AMERICAN	4½	5½	6½	7½	8½	9½	10½
CONTINENTAL	35	36	37	38	39	40	41

MEN'S COATS, JACKETS & SUITS

BRITISH	34	36	38	40	42	44
AMERICAN	34	36	38	40	42	44
CONTINENTAL	44	46	48	50	52	54

MEN'S SHOES

BRITISH	6	7	8	9	10	11
AMERICAN	7	8	9	10	11	12
CONTINENTAL	39½	40½	41½	42½	43½	44½

MEN'S SHIRTS

BRITISH	14	14½	15	15½	16	16½	17	17½
AMERICAN	14	14½	15	15½	16	16½	17	17½
CONTINENTAL	36	37	38	39	40	41	42	43

CHILDREN'S CLOTHING

AGE	3	5	7	8	9	10
BRITISH (HEIGHT)	40in	45in	50in	53in	55in	58in
CONTINENTAL (HEIGHT)	120cm	130cm	140cm	145cm	150cm	155cm

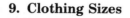

9. Clothing Sizes

SIZE	BUST METRIC	BUST IMPERIAL	WAIST METRIC	WAIST IMPERIAL	HIPS METRIC	HIPS IMPERIAL
10	83cm	32½in	64cm	25in	88cm	34½in
12	87cm	34in	67cm	26½in	92cm	36in
14	92cm	36in	71cm	28in	97cm	38in
16	97cm	38in	76cm	30in	102cm	40in
18	102cm	40in	81cm	32in	107cm	42in

DRESS PATTERN SIZES

METRIC	IMPERIAL
90cm	35/36in
100cm	39in
115cm	44/45in
120cm	48in
140cm	54/56in
150cm	60in
180cm	72in

FABRIC WIDTHS

10. Dress Patterns, Fabric Widths

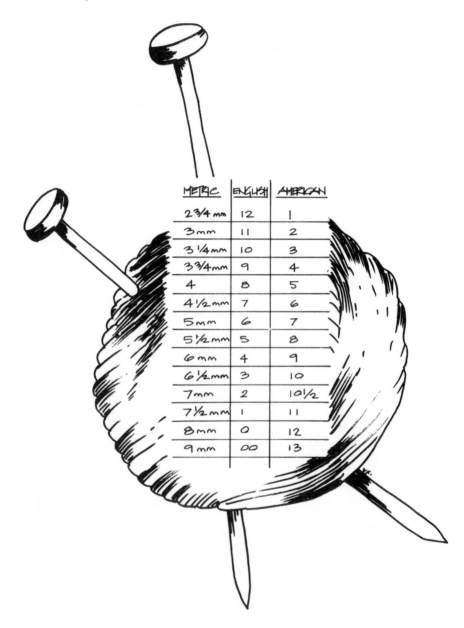

METRIC	ENGLISH	AMERICAN
2¾ mm	12	1
3 mm	11	2
3¼ mm	10	3
3¾ mm	9	4
4	8	5
4½ mm	7	6
5 mm	6	7
5½ mm	5	8
6 mm	4	9
6½ mm	3	10
7 mm	2	10½
7½ mm	1	11
8 mm	0	12
9 mm	00	13

11. Knitting Needle Sizes

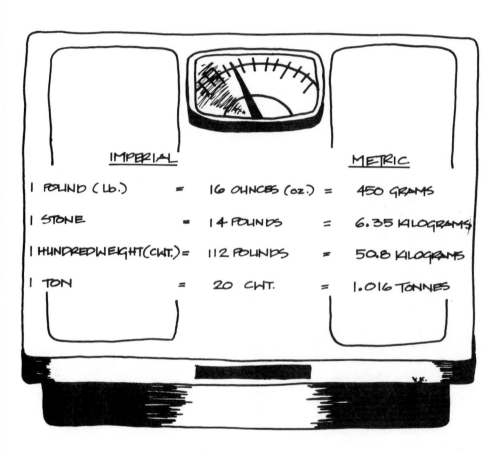

	IMPERIAL			METRIC
1 POUND (Lb.)	=	16 OUNCES (oz.)	=	450 GRAMS
1 STONE	=	14 POUNDS	=	6.35 KILOGRAMS
1 HUNDREDWEIGHT(CWT.)	=	112 POUNDS	=	50.8 KILOGRAMS
1 TON	=	20 CWT.	=	1.016 TONNES

12. Body Weight (stone, pounds, kilograms)

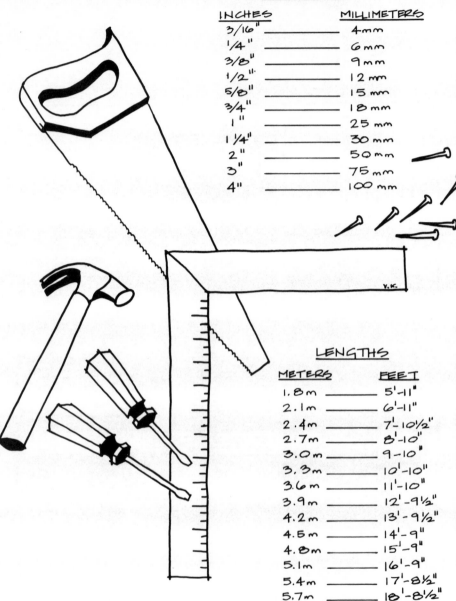

THICKNESS

INCHES	MILLIMETERS
3/16"	4mm
1/4"	6mm
3/8"	9mm
1/2"	12 mm
5/8"	15 mm
3/4"	18 mm
1"	25 mm
1 1/4"	30 mm
2"	50 mm
3"	75 mm
4"	100 mm

LENGTHS

METERS	FEET
1.8m	5'-11"
2.1m	6'-11"
2.4m	7'-10½"
2.7m	8'-10"
3.0m	9'-10"
3.3m	10'-10"
3.6m	11'-10"
3.9m	12'-9½"
4.2m	13'-9½"
4.5m	14'-9"
4.8m	15'-9"
5.1m	16'-9"
5.4m	17'-8½"
5.7m	18'-8½"

Y.K.

13. Lumber Sizes

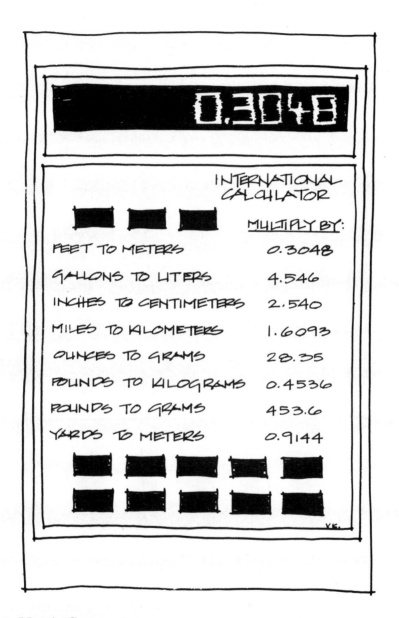

14. Metric Conversions

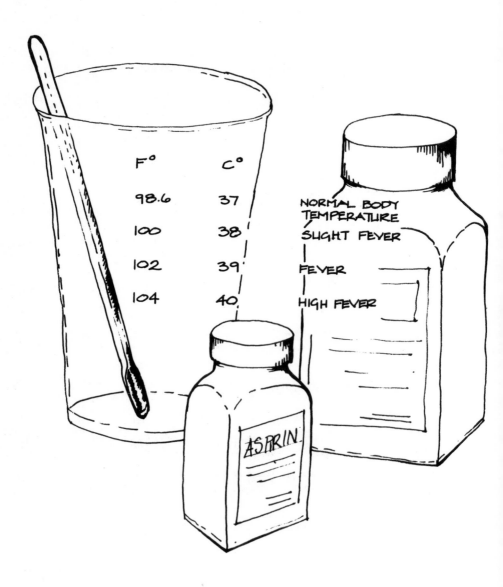

15. Fever Thermometer

CHAPTER 8

Food: How To Find It and Fix It

HOW TO SHOP FOR FOOD

The task of food shopping will at first seem to expand, filling all your waking moments. Familiarize yourself with the products available, and the time spent on this activity will soon shrink back to its normal size.

Milk

Your milkman offers services and goods at your door so wide-ranging that he almost deserves a new name. He may supply you with fresh turkeys, frozen meat, boxed wines, bread, fruit juices, eggs, potatoes, and even Christmas hampers! He probably delivers every day, maybe even on Sunday. Order your milk by color — the color of the cap, that is:

Pasteurized milk (silver cap). Minimum butter fat content 3%.

Homogenized milk (red cap). Same as pasteurized but has no cream line.

Skimmed milk (probably blue cap). Less than 0.3% butterfat. (Semi-skimmed, usually a striped cap, contains about 1.5% butterfat).

Long Life or UHT (Ultra Heat Treated) milk (pink cap). Keeps for several months unopened, as does sterilized milk. All of the other kinds of milk spoil quickly, even when refrigerated.

Channel Islands and South Devon milk (gold cap). More than 5% butterfat.

Cream (listed in ascending order of fat content, calories, and lusciousness):

Half cream. 12% butterfat. Use in coffee. Cannot be whipped.

Single cream. 18% butterfat. Pour over any dessert in the English way. Cannot be whipped.

Soured cream. 18% butterfat.

Whipping cream. 35% butterfat.

Double cream. 48% butterfat. Pour over each and every dessert, or whip (just a few flicks of the fork is enough).

Clotted cream. 55% butterfat. Use instead of butter on scones, with strawberry jam.

Cheese

Caerphilly (say kerFILLee). A mild white cheese, originally from Wales. Although it doesn't spread like cream cheese, use it as a tasty substitute in recipes.

Cheddar. Named for a small village in Somerset. Firm, crumbly, and a Mouse favorite in the kitchen. Look for Farmhouse Cheddar for a matured cheese with a rich musty flavor, but use Mild Cheddar in recipes calling for unspecified grated cheese.

Cheshire. The oldest of the cheeses, has a slightly salty taste. It is red, white, or blue, depending on the vegetable dye used.

Derby (say DARby). When seasoned with sage, a traditional Christmas cheese.

Double Gloucester (rhymes with "foster"). A strong, golden cheese with a matching strong, golden taste.

Lancashire (say LANKashur). A smooth-textured cooking cheese.

Leicester (say LESter). A reddish cheese with a fresh taste.

Stilton. A blue-veined cheese, goes well with port. Buy a wheel and pour port over it before serving.

Wensleydale. Now changing its color from blue to white, it goes well with fruit or apple pie.

Write to the **Cheese Board** for information and recipes using English cheese:

> The English Country Cheese Council, Dept. CWP
> 5-7 John Princes Street
> London W1
> tel. 01-499 7822

Eggs

Most eggs are brown (a fact of no importance, except at Eastertime, when you'll find them harder to dye) and are graded according to size. Size 1 is the largest, size 7 the smallest, and 3 and 4 are average.

Bread

You can get your bread just about any way you want it! It can be white, wholemeal, brown, wheatmeal, granary, or bran-enriched. It can be wrapped or unwrapped, sliced or unsliced. And the shapes of the loaves themselves are just as varied. Order them from the baker by name:

Barrel. Also known by such colorful names as Pistol, Rasp, Lodger's Loaf, or Crinkled Musket!

Bloomer. A popular loaf, nice and crusty because of the slashes on top. Also available in wholemeal.

Cob. Look for the sprinkling of crushed wheat on top.

Coburg. A crusty white bread, easily recognizable by the two slits on top that form a crown.

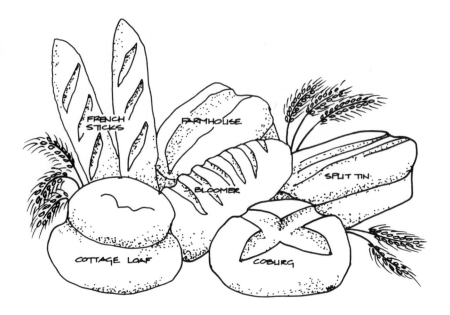

Cottage. A "double decker" dating back to Roman times.

French stick. Wholemeal as well as white.

Split tin. A long loaf, good size for sandwiches. The Farmhouse is shorter and fatter, giving larger slices.

Send away for recipes using bread as the main ingredient, including such dishes as Gipsy Pudding, Bangkok Bake, Mariner's Toast, and Schoolboy's Sizzler:

Flour Advisory Bureau, Bread Recipes
21 Arlington Street
London SW1
tel. 01-493 2521

Meat

Beef. Scotch beef has the best taste, or at least the best reputation. For lean ground beef, buy either *lean mince* or minced steak. A *skirt* *steak* is the same as flank steak. For barbecues, try fillet (say FILLit) or entrecote steaks, both very lean, or rump steak, a cheaper but tastier cut. If these steak cuts look too thin to you, don't hesitate to ask your butcher to cut you thicker slices. A roast, whether on or off the bone, is called a *joint*.

1. **Hind leg.** Stew slowly because of high gristle content.

2. **Topside and silverside.** Good for pot roast.

3. **Rump steak.** Broil, fry, or barbecue.
   Fillet steak. Broil, fry, or barbecue. Sometimes included as part of the sirloin.
   Sirloin steak. Fry, broil, quick roast, or barbecue. Steaks can be taken from any part of the sirloin; pieces cut from the upper part are best for broiling.

4. **Fore rib.** Quick roast. If boned and rolled, makes a good Sunday joint.
   Middle rib, thick rib. Slow roasting.

5. **Chuck steak.** Pot roast, braise, or stew.

6. **Neck.** Stew, use suet for making pastry.

7. **Clod.** Stew, good for pot roast, use suet for making pastry.

8. **Shin or foreleg.** Stew, use for stock.

9. **Brisket.** Usually boned and rolled for slow roasting, or braise.

10. **Thick flank, middle flank.** Slow roast, pot roast, braise.
    Thin flank. Stew.

Pork. There is profusion (and confusion) enough in the cured pork world. **Bacon** will come in all sorts of unrecognizable cuts, but for the familiar breakfast slice, ask for *rashers,* without rind. **Gammon** refers to the most expensive cut of bacon, sold in large pieces, like roasts, for baking or boiling. (To reduce saltiness, soak for 24 hours before roasting.) **Ham** is cut from the hindleg of the pig, when the pork is still uncured. There are many different cures; start your experimenting with York or Bradenham ham.

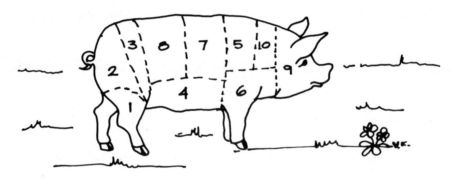

1. **Leg (knuckle end).** Score skin and roast. Can also be pickled and then boiled.

2. **Leg (fillet end).** Score skin and roast. The skin makes delicious crackling.

3. **Chump chops.** Broil, fry, bake.

4. **Belly.** Roll, stuff, and roast. Mix with leaner meats and stew.

5. **Spare ribs.** Roast or barbecue. Ask your butcher to leave the ribs connected, in one impressive slab.

6. **Hand.** Score skin and roast.

7. **Fore loin.** Roast. When cut into chops, broil, fry, braise, or bake.

8. **Hind loin.** Roast. Often sold as a chop with kidney attached.

9. **Head.** Stew, use for stock.

10. **Blade bone.** Roast, or marinate and barbecue.

Lamb. For a treat to remember, try English spring lamb. New Zealand lamb is readily available and less expensive.

1. **Best end of neck.** Broil, fry, or roast.

2. **Breast.** Slow roast, stew, or braise, after trimming excess fat.

3. **Breast.** When boned and rolled, makes an excellent stuffed roast.

4. **Chump chops.** Broil or fry.

5. **Cutlets.** Broil or fry, whether on the bone or boned and rolled.

6. **Gigot chops.** A Scottish term. Broil or fry.

7. **Leg.** Roast. Grind the leftovers and use in *cottage pie*.

8. **Loin.** Roast. The saddle of lamb includes the entire back of the lamb, from the neck to the end of the loin, and often the kidneys.

9. **Loin chops.** Broil, fry, or braise.

10. **Middle neck.** Stew.

11. **Rib chops.** Stew.

12. **Scrag end of neck.** Stew.

13. **Shank.** Stew.

14. **Shoulder.** Roast.

Veal

1. **Best end of neck.** Broil, fry, slow roast, or braise.

2. **Breast.** When boned and rolled, slow roast or braise. Stew when on the bone.

3. **Fillet.** Broil, fry.

4. **Knuckle.** Boil, stew, or use in meat pie. Bone and stuff, then slow roast or braise.

5. **Leg.** Roast, either on the bone or boned and stuffed.

6. **Loin.** Roast. Also good for kebabs.

7. **Scrag end of neck.** Stew.

8. **Shoulder.** Bone, dice, and use in stews, or roast.

Fish. Most fish are available all year, but quality varies with the season. When buying fresh fish, look for brightness. The eyes will be prominent, the scales sparkling, and the gills red. Ask the fishmonger to skin and dress the fish until you're adept at it.

Bass. A white fish. Best quality May through August.

Cod. A white fish. Quality lowest in summer months.

Flounder. A white fish, part of the plaice family. Best September through February.

Haddock. A white fish, part of the cod family. Buy whole or in fillets.

Herring. A small oily fish. When whole, brush with butter and grill or fry. When smoked, called *kippers*.

Mackerel. Delicious smoked.

Plaice. The most popular fish. Can be substituted for the more expensive sole in recipes.

Salmon. Sold whole or as steaks. Best during June, July, and August. Also available smoked.

Sole. Dover sole, the delicacy among white fish. Quality lowest in March and April.

Turbot. Similar to halibut.

Whiting. Part of the cod family, tasty but very bony.

Shellfish

Clams. Best September through November. Serve raw or cook like mussels.

Cockles. Usually available cooked and shelled.

Crab. Best in spring and summer. Usually boiled by the fishmonger. He may also dress it for you.

Lobster. Best April through August. Almost always sold cooked. Delicious!

Mussels. Sold live. Rinse, then boil in wine and herbs. Throw away the ones that don't open during cooking. Or, order a steamy pan full in the pub.

Oysters. Best in months with an R. Mainly from Cornwall.

Prawns (shrimp). Usually sold cooked, in all sizes: good all year round.

Scallops. Lowest quality May through August. Remove from shell and poach in wine.

Whelks, winkles. Traditional London treats, usually served cooked and cold. Use a pin to prise the little winkles out of their shells.

Game. Fresh game generally becomes available in the fall as the hunters go out, although you may find venison as early as July. The following are easily available, so add them to your diet: duck, grouse, hare, partridge, pheasant, pigeon, quail, rabbit, and venison.

Fruits: Soft Fruits Grown in England

Soft fruit include the small, stoneless fruits, such as most berries. Besides the familiar strawberries, blackberries, and blueberries, try the following:

Bilberry. A member of the blueberry family.

Black currants. Ideal for jams and pie fillings because of high pectin content.

Gooseberries. Generally unavailable outside Europe. Trim off both stem and bud end *(top and tail)* with scissors. Add plenty of sugar for an ideal pie filling.

Red currants. Very tart but delicious mixed with other, sweeter fruits. Clean berries from stem by running a fork down it.

For the freshest soft fruits, pick your own. These farms (and many more like them) are easily accessible to the Country Mouse and makes a nice day excursion for the City Mouse.

Crockford Bridge Farm
New Haw Road
Addlestone, Surrey
tel. Weybridge (0932) 54886

Southwood Fruit Farm
Burhill Road
Hersham, Surrey
tel. Walton-on-Thames (0932) 220808

For a complete listing of pick-your-own farms, request a copy of the
Farm Fresh Cookbook from the following organization:

Farm Shop and Pick your own Association (FSPA)
Hunger Lane
Muggington, Derby DE6 4PL
tel. Derby (0332) 360991

Other Fruits Grown in England

Apples. Try some unfamiliar eating apples, such as Cox's Orange
Pippin, Crispin, or Granny Smith. Worcesters have beautiful red
skins. The best cooking apple is the large Bramley.

Cherries. Use the sour Morello cherries for pies.

Pears. The most popular kinds are Comice, Conference, and
Williams.

Plums. Try the green Greengage or the purple Damson.

Quinces. Cannot be eaten raw, but delicious as jelly.

Imported Fruits. Fruits are imported from the farthest corners of
the world throughout the year. Bananas, coconuts, grapes, melons,
and pineapples are always available.

Citrus Fruits. The usual citrus fruits, such as oranges, lemons,
limes, and grapefruit, are imported all year. In the winter, look for
these two members of the tangerine family: Clementines (with seeds
and a thin rind) and Satsumas (seedless and easy to peel).

Cranberries. Available around Christmastime.

Figs. Although dried figs are always for sale, fresh figs are available in April through December.

Mangoes. They have a hard skin and a large pit. Use raw as a dessert fruit. Available except in October, November, and December.

Pawpaws (papayas). Available May through December. Serve like melons.

Peaches. Available June through December.

Vegetables

The common vegetables are easily available fresh at the usual times. Some familiar vegetables go under unfamiliar names, like the following: *aubergine* (eggplant), *beetroot* (beets), *calabrese* (broccoli), *courgette* (small zucchini), *marrow* (large zucchini).

The following vegetables may be unfamiliar to you, but try them:

Asparagus. Available in the spring. Although the green asparagus is more familiar, try the white variety, a true delicacy. Peel slightly before boiling. To eat, hold by the stem and dip into melted butter, or serve cold with Hollandaise sauce.

Belgian endive. Slice and serve raw in salads (including Waldorf salad) or braise in white wine and serve with butter.

Broad beans. Cook in the pod when young and tender. Shell when older and prepare like lima beans.

Runner beans. Similar to a stringy green bean.

Celeriac. Celery root. Add to soups or to your mashed potatoes.

Fennel. Delicate anise flavor. Trim both ends and boil.

Salsify. A root vegetable, also called *oyster plant*. Scrub, peel, and boil for as long as half an hour.

Swede. A round root vegetable, like a Swedish turnip.

FOOD LIST

The following foods and ingredients may be unknown to you or they may be old favorites parading under unfamiliar names. In cooking, apply your general philosophy of adopt and adapt, you'll soon feel at home with these ingredients.

British term	Equivalents, general remarks
Baking powder	If dissatisfied with the leavening of English baking powder, make your own: ¼ t. baking soda + ½ t. cream of tartar = 1 t. baking powder.
Bicarbonate of soda	Baking soda.
Bangers	Sausages.
Baps	Soft rolls. Use for sandwich or hamburger rolls.
Biscuits	Cookies. Try a *digestive biscuit* with your next cup of coffee and you'll be addicted.
Chips	French fries. Serve with deep fat fried fish for an English meal of *fish 'n chips*.
Chocolate, plain or bitter	Plain chocolate is semisweet; even "bitter" contains some sugar. For Baker's chocolate, use cocoa and butter: 3T cocoa + 1T butter = 1 square of Baker's chocolate. Use *Scotchbloc* for cake decorating.
Cling film	Plastic refrigerator wrap.
Cornflour	Cornstarch.
Crackers	Not only a good accompaniment for cheese, but a party favor to pull for a noisy Christmas celebration.
Crisps	Potato chips, in many flavors, including prawn, cheese, and salt 'n vinegar.
Digestive biscuits	Plain sugar cookies. Use for crumb crusts.
Fish fingers	Fish sticks, a children's favorite at "tea time."
Flan case	Pie shell.
Flour	Use *plain flour* for an all-purpose flour. *Self-raising* flour contains its own leavening agent.

Frankfurter	Hotdog.
Gentlemen's Relish	Officially known as *Patum Peperium,* this is a startling concoction of anchovies, butter, and herbs. Spread very thin on hot toast. Buy a miniature porcelain pot of it for the gentleman in your life.
Golden Syrup	Use this cane syrup as a substitute for corn syrup in recipes, reducing sugar slightly. Spread on toast and scones; drizzle on ice cream and baked apples; add to hot breakfast cereal, or even pancakes and waffles.
Ice lolly	Popsicle.
Jelly	Flavored gelatine (Jello) available in a gummy concentrate, rather than a powder, but can be substituted in your recipes. Reduce sugar somewhat.
Maize meal	Cornmeal.
Marmite	A dark brown herb concentrate. Spread on bread, very thinly if you treasure your tastebuds!
Pastry case	Pie shell.
Pimms #1	High-proof mixture of gin and flavorings. Dilute to taste with gingerale, soda water, etc. Add thin slices of fruit or cucumber.
Polkadots	Chocolate chips from Lyons.
Prawns	Shrimp.
Pudding	Dessert of any kind, whether actually a pudding or not.
Rasher	Slice of bacon.
Sandwich tin	Cake pan.
Scones	Similar to baking powder biscuits. The possibilities of this fattening temptation are discussed under Teas in this chapter.
Sorbet	Sherbet.
Squash	Add water to this liquid fruit concentrate for the nearest thing to Kool Aid.
Suet	Fat used in pastry for meat pies.
Sugar	Granulated sugar may be coarser than you

	are used to; for finer sugar use *castor sugar.* Sprinkle *demerara sugar,* crunchy and brown, on your cereal. *Vanilla sugar* has a faint vanilla flavor, for cooking. Confectioners sugar is called *icing sugar.*
Sultanas	Large amber-colored raisins; currants are darker and smaller. It all depends on the original grape.
Sweets	Candy and dessert.
Treacle	A dark sugar syrup that makes a good substitute for molasses. Make an old-fashioned treacle tart.
Yeast	1T dried yeast = one yeast cake = ½ ounce dried yeast = 25 grams fresh yeast, enough to raise 1½ pounds of flour.

WHERE TO SHOP FOR FOOD

It won't be long before you've chosen your favorite local shops, where the butcher will cut your meat the way you're used to, and bread is sold still warm from the oven. Watch out for unexpected closing times (perhaps Monday morning and Wednesday afternoon) and don't forget to bring your own shopping bag *(carrier bag).* Service is personal and courteous — just listen to the flurry of "thank you's" that accompany the exchange of money!

Supermarkets

For basics, try these popular supermarket chains: Safeway, Sainsbury's, Waitrose, and Tesco. W.H. Cullen, also a chain, carries a luxury range of imported delicatessen items, a full range of cheese, and good frozen foods, including top quality Loseley Farm ice cream. Don't expect help with packing at the checkout counter. The cashier is in charge of the cash register *(till)* and your receipt *(till slip),* but not much else.

Food Halls

Department stores offer a large range in their food halls. **Marks and Spencers** has a good basic food department and their chicken is of high quality. **Harrods Food Halls** are so luxurious that it's easy to forget how well stocked they are in basics, too. Try them for your daily bread (serve yourself) as well as for the occasional treat. **Selfridges** has just as large a choice, even if the setting is less glamorous. For old-fashioned delicacies that come in cans and boxes (and hampers, of course) try **Fortnum and Mason** on Piccadilly. Stop outside this store on the hour as the clock strikes. Could that be the proper Mr. Fortnum and the portly Mr. Mason?

Imported Food Shops

Until you and the rest of your family wean yourselves away from the food you've been accustomed to, make a trip to one of these shops with old familiar brand names on the shelves. They are less than an hour's drive for the City Mouse.

Antons
101 Hare Lane
Claygate (near Esher), Surrey
tel. Esher (0372) 62306

Hampers
121 Hersham Road
Walton-on-Thames, Surrey
tel. Walton-on-Thames (0932) 43541

Cheese Shops

Try this traditional shop for good cheese and old-fashioned courtesy:

Paxton and Whitfield
93 Jermyn Street
London SW1
tel. 01-903 9892

The Swiss Centre will grate and mix cheese for your **cheese fondue.** Just tell them how many you need to serve.

Swiss Centre
2 New Coventry Street
London W1
tel. 01-734 1291

Cheddar cheese is made in the Mendip Hills. Cylinders still in the rind and wrapped in cheesecloth can be ordered by mail. Cheese is heavy, so watch the postage!

Chewton Cheese Dairy
Priory Farm
Chewton Mendip
tel. Chewton Mendip (076 121) 560

Frozen Food

Bejam's, a chain selling frozen food, with branches in just about every High Street, has a large selection, well-displayed in separate freezers, including turkeys for the holidays. There you can buy other basics in bulk, such as wine and party supplies. They will deliver large orders.

Health Food

In addition to a good supply of organic food, grains, and every other ingredient needed for healthy baking, Cranks have several restaurants offering tasty vegetarian lunches, in Heal's and Peter Robinson's department stores and at this address:

Cranks Health Foods
Marshall Street
London W1
tel. 01-437 2915

Holland & Barrett have many branches, over 22 in London alone. These two are centrally located:

Holland & Barrett
220 Fulham Road
London SW10
tel. 01-351 3904

High Street, St. John's Wood
London NW8
tel. 01-586 5494

Liquor Store

A liquor store is called an *off licence* — logically, because their license allows them to sell alcohol to be consumed off the premises. They are usually open seven days a week, with Sunday hours resembling pub hours. A well-equipped off licence may sell ice cubes by the bag, rent glasses, and supply other party necessities.

HOW TO EAT ENGLISH AND BAKE BRITISH

English food has a nasty reputation which, like that of English weather, is largely undeserved. English food is much more than greasy sausages, frozen peas, and dishes with unappetizing names like Toad in the Hole or Bubble and Squeak. If you are selective in your choice of restaurants and cooking ingredients, English food will come to mean things like delicious cream so thick you can whip it easily with a fork, spring lamb, and pick-your-own fresh strawberries.

To eat your way through the day in a very English way, start with a **prebreakfast cup of tea** while reading your morning newspaper. To a late, brunch-like breakfast, add **kippers** (smoked herring) basted with butter and grilled; **sausages** (the best are Oxford sausages, still made there); and **grilled tomatoes**.

The coffee ritual of **elevenses**, named for the morning hour when it takes place, is faithfully adhered to, whether you're at home or out of the house. Stop where you see the Rombouts sign for an excellent cup of drip coffee. At home, invite your neighbor in for half an hour. If she'd like her coffee *white,* add milk (not cream).

Homemade cookies *(biscuits)* are not necessary; serve digestive biscuits or some other plain cookie.

Lunch is often a hot meal, with meat, potatoes, and a vegetable. Your children can choose to eat the hot lunch served at their English schools, and their playmates will expect a hot meal when invited to your house.

Sunday lunch, contrary to its name, is not a bite taken on the run before family members depart for their various activities, but a proper dinner eaten at about one o'clock. For a typical Sunday lunch, serve a roast *(joint)*, Yorkshire pudding, roast potatoes, and for dessert *(pudding)* a fruit trifle or fruit crumble. Of course, the tastiest lunch available can be found down the road at the pub! This is described in mouth-watering detail in Chapter 13 on pubs.

Tea, although a simple enough word, has many complicated meanings. It can mean anything from a *cuppa* on the run to an elegant spread served to company. Offer a cup of tea to anyone entering your door, including workmen, particularly between 3:30 and 5:30 in the afternoon. Ask your guests if they'd like it with milk (you add it for them, after pouring in the tea) or a slice of lemon. Let them help themselves to sugar. Restaurant tea is such a strong brew that you may want to use the accompanying pot of hot water (meant for the second round) to dilute it. Both tea and coffee will be served containing milk unless you have specifically ordered them without.

Afternoon tea can be as formal as you dare to make it. Eat it in the living room, everyone balancing plates and cups on laps. You can serve a selection of sweets like **crumpets** (toasted under the broiler and served warm with butter dripping into the holes), **English muffins** (here called simply "muffins," of course), **sponge** (a white cake with whipped cream and jam between the layers), or best of all, warm **scones** from your oven.

When traveling or walking, follow the signs announcing **Cream Tea**. You will probably be served a set tea that includes an assortment of sandwiches, cakes, and scones. The mound on the top of your scone is the "cream" in the Cream Tea.

High tea can be a family occasion and a nice time to invite other families with children to visit. It is eaten from five o'clock onward. The menu is so varied that there is something for almost every age. Besides the sweet things mentioned above, serve non-sweet dishes like sandwiches (cucumber, watercress, smoked salmon) on thin delicate slices, eggs in some cold form, a variety of cheese, or some interesting salads.

To confuse matters even further, **tea** also means a simple hot meal served in the evening to children (a leftover from nursery days with Nanny?). Ironically, at this meal, not a drop of tea can be found!

Dinner or supper means familiar food, but it is eaten later than you're probably used to, about 7:30.

How To Give a Dinner Party

When giving a dinner party, your mother's sensible advice about just being yourself and acting naturally will carry you a long way. But try introducing some English touches:

Invite your dinner guests using convenient British wording: *eight for eight-thirty*. Guests are expected to arrive promptly at 8:00, so that you can serve dinner at 8:30 sharp.

At the door, you will receive a traditional hostess gift of wine or flowers and a kiss on the cheek, from either or both sexes.

Offer sherry, Scotch, Martini (sweet vermouth), wine, or gin and tonic to drink. Forget the fancy cocktails, which are not very popular, but do try a fruit punch, which is. Keep the accompanying nibbles simple and the cocktail "hour" short.

The table setting is familiar, with these exceptions: there is usually no water goblet or salad plate, but often a bread-and-butter plate. Dessert silverware *(cutlery)* is at the top of the plate, with the spoon above the fork. The bowl of the spoon points left, the tines of the fork point right.

Choose the topics of conversation with care. Avoid any subjects even remotely related to status; for example, don't even mention your job, its perks, your education, or the brilliant accomplishments of your children.

Serve as many courses as you have courage, energy, and tableware for. Salad as a separate course is served after the main course; cheese can be eaten either before dessert (the French way) or after it (the English way). In a domestic version of the sweets trolley found in restaurants, there should be two or three choices of dessert.

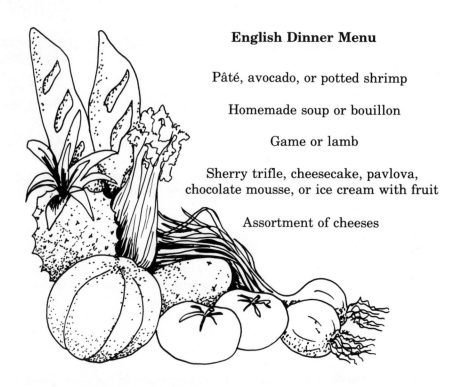

English Dinner Menu

Pâté, avocado, or potted shrimp

Homemade soup or bouillon

Game or lamb

Sherry trifle, cheesecake, pavlova,
chocolate mousse, or ice cream with fruit

Assortment of cheeses

Expect a polite phone call the next day from your grateful guests.
Don't forget to make it sound as though the whole project was a
cinch. It was, wasn't it?

WELL-KNOWN ENGLISH DISHES

Slowly add some English dishes to your repertoire, starting with
these five basics:

Fish and chips. Both are deep fat fried but need not be greasy.
Make a light batter for the fish, using beer or water (not milk).
Make French fries, and serve them authentically wrapped in
newspaper, sprinkled with vinegar!

Scone (rhymes with "gone" and not "lone"). It's a near relative of the American baking powder biscuit. Picture yourself on a rainy Sunday, reading by the fire, and at four o'clock, scones fresh from the oven. Serve them warm, split, spread with butter, strawberry jam, and clotted cream. Then go for a brisk walk!

Steak and kidney pie is a deep-dish pie using cubes of lean beef, slices of veal kidney, and mushrooms, covered with a suet pastry crust. To keep your crust from getting soggy, cook the meat and gravy mixture separately before covering with pastry. Serve directly from the casserole dish; for fancy occasions, wrap a white napkin around it.

Trifle. There are almost as many recipes for this Victorian dessert as there are English cooks, and you'll soon develop your own. Think in these layers: first ladyfingers or sponge cake, drenched with sherry (or any available booze) and spread with jam; then a layer of fresh fruit, a layer of vanilla custard, a layer of Jello *(jelly),* a layer of whipped cream, and a sprinkling of almonds or angelica. Be creative; proportions and exact ingredients are entirely up to you. Assemble it in a glass dish so that the layers are visible, and be sure to dig right to the bottom when serving.

Yorkshire pudding, contrary to its name, is not a dessert, but a light breadlike accompaniment to a roast. The batter, similar to that used for popovers, is poured into the hot pan juices, either together with the roast during the last minutes of cooking or after the roast has been removed. Serve immediately.

HOW TO FOLLOW AN ENGLISH RECIPE

In an English recipe, dry ingredients are measured according to weight, so invest in a convenient kitchen scale. Liquid ingredients are based on the Imperial pint, which is 20 fluid ounces (instead of 16), so add a glass measuring cup with Imperial measures to your equipment. For further measuring equivalents, see the charts in Chapter 7 on measurements.

If an English recipe calls for ... **Use this American equivalent measure**

	Imperial	Metric	U.S.
breadcrumbs	4 ounces	100 grams	1 cup
butter	1 ounce	25 grams	2 heaping Tbsp.
	4 ounces	100 grams	½ cup plus 1 Tbsp.
cornstarch	1 ounce	25 grams	3 heaping Tbsp.
flour	1 ounce	25 grams	¼ cup
	8 ounces	200 grams	2 cups
golden syrup, treacle	1 ounce	25 grams	1 Tbsp.
milk, other liquids	2 fl. ounces	50 milliliters	¼ cup
	8 fl. ounces	225 milliliters	1 cup
	16 fl. ounces	450 milliliters	2 cups (U.S. pint)
	1 pint (20 ounces)	550 milliliters	2¼ cups
nuts	4 ounces	100 grams	1 cup
raisins	2 ounces	50 grams	⅓ cup
rice	4 ounces	100 grams	⅔ cup
sugar, granulated	1 ounce	25 grams	2 Tbsp.
	8 ounces	200 grams	1 cup
sugar, confectioners	1 ounce	25 grams	¼ cup
	4 ounces	100 grams	1 cup
sugar, brown	2 ounces	50 grams	⅓ cup, packed
yeast	½ ounce, dried	25 grams, fresh	1 cake

CHAPTER 9

How To Get There: Transportation and Travel

THE CAR

Drivers License

When you become a resident of Britain, you have one year in which to acquire a British *driving licence*. If you hold a valid license from one of the Common Market countries, it is a simple matter of forfeiting your present license and receiving a new British one. For others, the transaction is not so simple. You must take a series of tests: an eye test, an oral test on the Highway Code, and a half-hour driving test. The sooner you face this terrible fact and start to work, the better, for there may be delays at every stage. The method of attack:

Step 1.

Buy a copy of *The Highway Code* from your bookshop. Memorize the rules and traffic signs. For further information on this fascinating subject, request a free copy of *Your Driving Test* from the DVLC:

> DVLC (Driver and Vehicle Licensing Centre)
> Driver Enquiry Unit
> Swansea SA6 7JL
> tel. Swansea (0792) 72151

Step 2.

Request Form DL 26 at the post office to apply for a driving license. (There may be a delay of weeks now, so you will have plenty of time to tackle steps 3 and 4 before your test.) Send in the completed form with the fee:

DVLC (Driver and Vehicle Licensing Centre)
First Application Section
Swansea SA99 1AD

Step 3.

Take a few driving lessons to pick up some special techniques even if you have been driving for years. One of the best known of the many companies offering instruction is the British School of Motoring. Call them to find the branch nearest you.

The British School of Motoring
tel. 01-540 8262 (head office)
tel. 01-785 9799 (regional office)

Step 4.

Practice driving around the town or area in which you are going to take your test. (The driving school may be willing to do this with you.)

Failed? Don't be discouraged. Wait a calendar month and take the test again — in fact, as many times as necessary to pass it — before the year has expired, of course, or else you will have to get a provisional driving license as a temporary measure.

Passed? Congratulations! You now have a driving license that expires the day before you turn 70!

Regulations, Recommendations, and Biased Comments

🐿 **Stay on the left side of the road.** Actually, this isn't too difficult to remember since you've got all those oncoming cars to remind you! Even more confusing may be a left-right reversal inside your car — your gear shift and light dimmer are on the left, your windshield *(windscreen)* wipers on the right. Console yourself — the positions of the clutch and brake pedals are not reversed!

🐿 Everyone in the front seat must wear a **seat belt.** This does not apply to backseat passengers.

🐿 **Roundabouts** deserve a chapter of their own. They are meant to keep traffic moving smoothly but some people regard them more as hurdles in a horse race — obstacles to be overcome on the way to a destination. Traffic already on the roundabout (which is coming from your right and going clockwise, remember) has right of way over traffic coming up to the roundabout. Get in the proper lane before entering the roundabout and use your left-hand direction signal when getting off. Have courage! After the first month, it will seem less intimidating and less like that other kind of roundabout at the fair.

🐿 **Speed limits** are 70 mph on *motorways* (highways designated with an M) and *dual carriageways* (divided highways); 60 mph on *single carriageways* (roads with a single lane in each direction). If no speed limit is posted, it is 30 mph.

🐿 Make way for **ambulances,** fire engines, and police with sirens, but you do not necessarily have to pull over and stop.

🐿 **Pedestrians** on the crosswalk *(zebra crossing)* have right of way as soon as they step onto it. (*Pelican crossings* have traffic lights to guide cars. Wait until the flashing yellow signal stops before driving on.)

🐿 **Pedestrians** should wait for the green man signal to cross the street. A series of high beeps will call your attention to this. Sprint across, as your time is limited.

🐿 **Do not pass** *(overtake)* before a pedestrian crossing marked by a pattern of zigzag lines.

🐿 At a **junction**, you must give right of way if there are double broken white lines across the road you are on. A Give Way sign or an inverted triangle also tells you to yield right of way.

🐿 The term **offside** refers to the driver's or right-hand side of the car. The side nearest the curb is the **nearside.**

🐿 If you see a sign saying *Headlamps Dipped,* dim your headlights.

🐿 **No parking** is ever allowed at double yellow lines along the curb *(kerb)*. A single yellow line prohibits parking during working hours on workdays.

🐭 You will be amazed to discover **bicycles** on highways and even more amazed to learn that they are there legally. They are prohibited only from *motorways* (designated with an M).

🐭 The **yellow traffic light** appears **before and after** red, apparently to give you a chance to shift into gear and get ready to go. (English drivers put their cars in neutral while waiting, with the hand brake on.) Do not proceed until the green light appears.

🐭 **Driving while intoxicated** (80 milligrams of alcohol to 100 milliliters of blood) will almost always result in loss of license for one year.

🐭 **Road signs** have white or yellow lettering on a dark green background. The route number in parentheses refers not to the road you are on but the one you will be led to.

🐭 **A car flashing its headlights** at you is the same as a man politely tipping his hat. He is saying, "After you, madam," and is helping you out of some awkward traffic situation. Thank him by waving graciously when your move has been executed.

🐭 Learn to read the **road surface** for all sorts of traffic directions — arrows, lines, and even words. The most important of these is the broken double line at the end of a road as it comes up to another, which means: give way to traffic on the major road. Be careful, even if you do not see a Stop or Yield sign; check the road surface before you take right of way.

🐭 **Parking**, particularly in London, is a nightmare. There is a whole maze of restrictions on parking — yellow lines may be single, double, or broken; they may run parallel or perpendicular to the curb *(kerb),* but they all mean, at the very least, that parking is prohibited during working hours. In general, the more lines, the more restricted the parking, but check on all the refinements yourself. The City Mouse may apply for a **Resident Parking Permit** at her Local Council, which will allow her to park in specially designated parking places in her borough.

🐭 The Country Mouse can make use of **Pay and Display**

multi-storey car parks. After parking on one of the levels of the parking garage, find a yellow automat, estimate generously how long you'll stay, and buy a ticket for that length of time. Stick this ticket to the inside of your windshield.

🐾 You must stop when you see a **Lollipop Lady** (crossing guard) holding her out-sized lollipop to allow school children to cross the road.

🐾 Your car, with its steering wheel on the right, is called a *right-hand drive,* even though you drive it on the left.

🐾 When driving in private streets in the country, drive slowly so as not to wake the **Sleeping Policemen.**

🐾 Don't drive in **bus lanes.** Do note the times posted, though, because some bus lanes are open to all traffic except during peak hours.

🐾 Don't sound your **horn** *(hooter)* in a built-up area between 11:30 p.m. and 7 a.m. In fact, exercise restraint in the use of your horn; you'll be pleasantly surprised to notice that even city traffic is quite quiet.

Traffic Signs

There are three categories of traffic signs. Signs giving orders are generally circles outlined in red. Warning signs are triangular and also rimmed in red. Direction signs are mostly rectangular; on the motorways they are blue with white lettering and on primary routes they have green backgrounds.

Driving Terms

It is crucial to eliminate the language barrier in driving terminology. Learn this vocabulary before going for your test:

British English	American English
amber (light)	yellow
bonnet	hood
boot	trunk
car park (multi-storey car park)	parking lot (parking garage)
cul-de-sac, close	dead-end street
diversion	detour
dynamo	generator
dual carriageway	divided highway
estate car	station wagon
flyover	overpass
gearbox	transmission
indicator	turn signal
kerb	curb
lay-by	place to pull off the road
lorry (articulated lorry)	truck (trailer truck)
motorway	freeway
to overtake	to pass
pavement	sidewalk
petrol	gas
registration number	license plate number
roundabout	traffic circle
saloon	sedan
silencer	muffler
verge	shoulder
windscreen	windshield

What To Do If You Have a Car Accident
(as advised by the Consumers' Association)

Keep a copy of these steps in the glove compartment to help you through the shock of having an accident:

1. **Stop.** The law requires you to stop and stay for a reasonable time. You must also give your name and address to anyone involved in or affected by the accident.

2. **Get the other driver's information:** name, address, phone

number, insurance company, make and license number of car.

3. **Write down** names and addresses of witnesses and their license numbers.

4. **Do not discuss what has happened.** If you admit liability, offer apologies or payment, or take the blame, your insurance company may refuse to settle.

5. **Call the police** if anyone has been injured, if you've damaged anyone's property (including animals), if you think the other driver has committed an offense, or if you are sure you are not to blame.

6. **Write down what has happened:** injuries to persons, damage to vehicles, state of traffic, weather and road surface conditions, identification of other vehicles involved, what was said.

7. **Make a sketch map** which includes direction of travel, position of cars, any skid marks, road signs, positions of witnesses.

Automobile Clubs

There are two main **automobile clubs,** the **AA** (Automobile Association) and the **RAC** (Royal Automobile Club). They offer similar services: 24-hour breakdown service, valuation of second-hand cars, reports on road conditions, travel advice, an excellent selection of road maps, and coverage abroad.

The Automobile Association (AA)
Fanum House, Basing View
Basingstoke
tel. Basingstoke (0256) 20123 (head office, not breakdown service)
tel. 01-954 7373 (breakdown service for the City Mouse)

The Automobile Association
Fanum House, 22 Friary Street
Guildford, Surrey
tel. Guildford (0483) 572841 (Country Mice outside of Surrey should enquire at the head office number given above for the AA office nearest them.)

The Royal Automobile Club (RAC)
83 Pall Mall
London SW1
tel. 01-839 7050 (head office for the City Mouse)

The Royal Automobile Club
PO Box 100
RAC House, Lansdowne Road
Croydon CR9 2JA
tel. 01-686 2525 (head office for the Country Mouse)
tel. Watford (92) 33555 (rescue services for London north of the
     Thames, Bedfordshire, Essex, Hertfordshire, Middlesex).
tel. 01-681 3611 (rescue services for London south of the Thames,
     Kent, Surrey, East and West Sussex)

MOT Test. Any car more than three years old must undergo a test
every year. This is known as an MOT: the letters stand for the
Ministry of Transport. You may have this inspection done at any
garage and they will issue you an MOT certificate, which you
present with proof of insurance when you pay road tax.

Road Tax is a standard fee paid every year on every vehicle,
whatever the age, size, or weight of the car. Pay at the post office
and receive a round sticker to be displayed on the inside of your
windshield.

THE TRAIN

The Country Mouse will probably use the train primarily as a
commuter service to reach London (see the map in Chapter 1 on
housing). British Rail, however, offers many more services. At their
Travel Centres, you can plan a trip, reserve your seat, get a sleeper,
even book a hotel room.

British Rail Travel Centres (no phone calls, open during office
     hours)

4-12 Lower Regent Street, London SW1

14 Kingsgate Parade, Victoria Street, London SW1

407 Oxford Street, London W1

87 King William Street, London EC4

Regular users of the train can save money by taking advantage of special offers. An **Annual Season Ticket** for the Country Mouse who works in London can save up to 40% in train fare, when the route is fixed. This can also include connecting Underground service. A **Family Railcard** permits up to four adults to travel for half fare, and up to four children for one pound each. The people traveling together do not have to be family members, and the card is good for a year. An **Awayday Return** offers a cheaper return ticket, valid for one day only, with some restrictions as to time of departure (usually after peak hours).

British Rail also offers **24-hour recorded information.** Use their *Dial-and-Listen* service listed in the white pages of the phone book under *British Rail.*

The **Inter-City trains** are fast (an average of 70 mph, with some up to 125 mph, and about 900 each day have a dining car. (To spot the dining car from the outside, look for the red stripe above the windows.)

Inter-City Europe connects you to over 140 continental cities, including transfer to ferry. There are **six inter-city** stations. You can phone them once your general destination is known:

Euston Station (to go to East Midlands, North Wales, or via the West Coast to Scotland): tel. 01-387 7070

King's Cross Station (to go to West Yorkshire, Northeast, or via the East Coast to Scotland): tel. 01-278 2477

Liverpool Street Station (to go to East Anglia and Essex): tel. 01-283 7171

Paddington Station (to go to West of England, West Midlands, South Wales): tel. 01-262 6767

St. Pancras Station (to go to East Midlands, South Yorkshire): tel. 01-387 7070

Waterloo Station (to go to Southeast, Southwest): tel. 01-928 5100

Avoid the cost of an overnight stay and take an **Inter-city Sleeper:**

for the luxury-minded, a first-class sleeper, or for the more practical, adjoining doubles to keep an eye on the Young Mice. Sleeper reservation offices:

Euston Station: tel. 01-387 8541

King's Cross Station: tel. 01-278 2411

Paddington Station: tel. 01-723 7000

If you need your car but don't want to drive it, take the **Motorail** and put your car on the train. There are year-round services to Aberdeen, Edinburgh, Newcastle, Penzance, Stirling, and Inverness. For information on Motorail:

Euston Station: tel. 01-387 8541

King's Cross Station: tel. 01-837 4200

Paddington Station: tel. 01-723 7000

At 73 **Rail Drive Stations** in England, you can arrange to have a rental car waiting at the station for you. For information, inquire at the Godfrey Davis Car Hire Kiosk at one of the main London train stations listed above or call their headquarters, tel. (Heathrow) 01-897 0811.

For sheer old-fashioned luxury take a trip on **The Orient Express.** Besides their well-known trip to the "orient," they offer Pullman Day Journeys within England.

The Venice Simplon-Orient-Express
Sea Containers House
20 Upper Ground
London SE1
tel. 01-928 5837

THE UNDERGROUND

London has an efficient web of subways known officially as **the Underground** and unofficially as *the tube.* (Don't be confused by signs saying *subway.* They direct you to an underground passageway for pedestrians — a safe way to cross a busy street. You might, in fact, take a subway to the Underground!)

Get your copy of the very clear Underground map at any station. Save your coins if you want to use the ticket machines to avoid delays at the ticket windows. Most trips will cost either 40 or 50 pence, depending on your destination. Children under 16 travel for half price; children under five and dogs of any age travel free. Don't misplace your ticket. You need it to get out of the Underground and into the daylight once more. There is no service after 12 midnight or before 5 in the morning. For further information, call London Transport: tel. 01-222 1234.

For **lost and found items:**

London Transport Lost Property Office
200 Baker Street
London NW1
tel. 01-486 2496 (24-hour answering service)

Visit the London Transport Museum to climb on old buses and to see a display of Underground maps from 1908 onward.

London Transport Museum
39 Wellington Street
London WC2
tel. 01-379 6344

THE BUS

Although your last experience with a bus may have been the big yellow school bus, don't reject this means of getting around in London and in the country.

The advantages of bus travel for the City Mouse are as clear as the view from the upper deck. Although buses generally stop running at midnight, there are infrequent night buses. Multi-colored maps are available free from Underground and bus stations. Fares are based on distance, as on the Underground. Red Arrow buses offer express service from main train stations and shopping districts.

The Country Mouse can use the Greenline Bus for travel into London or from town to town. For information and a booklet on their services:

London Country Bus Services Ltd. (The Greenline)
Bell Street
Reigate, Surrey RH2 7LE
tel. Reigate (07372) 42411

London Country Bus Services Ltd.
Eccleston Bridge
London SW1
tel. 01-834 5563

For longer trips in England and Wales, as well as transportation to Heathrow, Gatwick, and Luton airports, take one of the National Express Coaches. (A *coach* is bigger and fancier and covers greater distances than a mere bus.) Inquire at Victoria Coach Station:

Victoria Coach Station, Coach Service Inquiries
164 Buckingham Palace Road
London SW1
tel. 01-730 0202

AIRLINES AND AIRPORTS

Because you are now living on an island, you will find yourself turning to air travel more than ever. There are four airports conveniently close to London, the largest of which is **Heathrow**.

Heathrow Airport
Hounslow, Middlesex TW6 1JH
tel. 01-759 4321 (flight inquiries)

For arrival and departure information you can also call the specific terminal:

Terminal 1 (British and Irish airlines): 01-745 7702

Terminal 2 (European airlines): 01-745 7115

Terminal 3 (arrivals of intercontinental airlines): 01-745 7412
        (departures of intercontinental airlines):
            01-745 7067

You can also get flight information from specific airlines. These numbers are listed under *British Airports Authority* in the white pages of your phone book.

The City Mouse can get to Heathrow easily on the Underground, using the Piccadilly line. Allow at least 45 minutes. There are also regular bus services: take an Airbus from Victoria, Euston, or Paddington train station (tel. 01-222-1234); or catch a Flightline bus from Victoria to Heathrow, Gatwick, or Luton (tel. 01-730 0202).

The Country Mouse can get to Heathrow easily too, as there are special coaches, called Railair Link, from three train stations: Reading, Staines, and Woking.

Gatwick Airport is no longer a poor country cousin to Heathrow. It is modern and easy to get to, and it has regular service to 40 destinations daily.

Gatwick Airport
Horley, Surrey RH6 0NP
tel. 01-668 4211 (flight information; or see *British Airports Authority* in the phone book)

To get to Gatwick, the City Mouse can also take the fast **Gatwick Express** from Victoria Station. Trains leave every 15 minutes, are non-stop, travel at speeds up to 90mph, and arrive at Gatwick in half an hour. There are some other train connections from stations in the south — Croydon, Guildford, and Reading, among others.

To travel between Gatwick and Heathrow airports, take a direct, non-stop bus called **Jetlink 747**, which takes a good hour, or **Jetlink 727**, which stops on route and takes at least an hour and a half (tel. 01-730 0202). There is also helicopter service: ten round trips a day between airports.

The two other airports serving London are situated north of London:

Luton Airport
tel. Luton (0582) 36061
Stansted Airport
tel. Bishops Stortford (0279) 502380

Bucket shops, operating in the gray area of the law, are agencies that sell unofficially discounted air tickets. They do not usually include tickets to North America since so much price wrangling is already going on. Although these tickets are "unofficial," they are not illegal. You can find the shops with very legal-sounding names in the want ads of your newspaper.

Keep yourself informed about **cheap flights**. Call the following number for the best ticket value:

Air Travel Advisory Bureau
tel. 01-636 5000

FERRIES

The **car ferry** is a very practical way to get off your island home. The English Channel must be crowded with ferries scurrying back and forth, for your choice is wide and varied.
　　You can make reservations with a travel agent or contact these main ferry lines directly:

Olau Line: tel. Sheerness (0795) 666666

P & O Ferries: tel. 01-623 1505

Sealink: tel. 01-834 2345

Townsend Thoresen: tel. 01-734 4431

For the quicker crossing by hovercraft:

Hoverlloyd: tel. 01-499 9481

Hoverspeed: tel. 01-554 7061

Seaspeed: tel. 01-606 3681

Don't forget that, although Holland, Belgium, or France (the Mainland) will be your usual destination, ferries also take you to Ireland, the Channel Islands, Denmark, and even Sweden.

The main ports of departure from England

Dover	Newhaven
Felixstowe	Portsmouth
Folkestone	Sheerness
Harwich	Southampton

The main ports of arrival on the Continent

Belgium	**France**	**The Netherlands**
Ostend	Boulogne	Hook of Holland
Zeebrugge	Calais	Rotterdam
	Dunkerque	Vlissingen (Flushing)
	Dieppe	
	Cherbourg	
	Le Havre	

TAXIS

Black cabs, sometimes found in other conservative colors these days, can be hailed on the street. Make sure the *For Hire* sign is lighted; this means the cab is vacant. A generous 10% tip is strongly recommended. You can phone for a black cab. Both the Country Mouse and the City Mouse can find a complete listing in the white pages of the phone book under *Taxis*.

For lost property in a taxi, go to their office:
Taxi Lost Property Office
15 Panton Street
London NW1

CHAPTER 10

Money, Banking and Taxes

MONEY

Since 1971, English money has been based on the decimal system. Gone are the days of half-crowns and shillings. The basic unit is the pound (referred to in official circles as a *pound sterling* and in unofficial circles as a *quid*), which is divided into 100 units called *pence,* or simply *p.* for short. There are eight coins: ½, 1, 2, 5, 10, 20, and 50 pence, and one pound. Although you will quickly learn to spend these, note that value has little relationship to size, so that the new pound coin is smaller (but thicker) than most of the others, and the 10-pence coin is larger and much more impressive than the 20-pence coin. The 20-pence and the 50-pence coins are both seven-sided, with the 50-pence looking like a prosperous cousin of the smaller one.

If you get an old 5-pence coin, it will say *one shilling* from the days before the decimal system; it is still occasionally called a *bob.* Likewise, the old two-shilling piece is now a 10-pence coin.

The bills *(notes)*, in contrast to the coins, get larger as their face value increases, and their colors vary too. A young Queen Elizabeth is pictured on one side. The denominations of bills are £1, 5, 10, 20, and 50.

BANKS

There are four main banks, each with branches throughout England and Wales: Barclays Bank, Lloyds Bank, Midland Bank, and National Westminster (known to its friends as Nat West). These all offer similar services, as do the smaller banks. Banking hours are generally from 9:30 a.m. to 3:30 p.m. Monday through Friday, although some banks are also open on Saturday morning. There is one way to get around these rigid hours — the **cash dispenser**. The machines that are set in the outside wall of the bank can be used 24 hours a day, seven days a week. Go to any one of them connected with your bank, insert a special cash card, and punch in your personal number (both provided by your bank). Crisp new money is yours, up to the limit of around 100 pounds a day. Memorize your personal number, or at the very least, keep it separate from your cash card.

Open a **checking account** *(current account)* and get yourself a checkbook and a bank card. Fill out the check *(cheque)* in the familiar way, with these three small exceptions. First of all, don't forget to write the date correctly, with the day preceding the month: January the thirteenth is written 13-1-1986. Second, the money amount is written with a dash instead of a decimal point: ten pounds, 70 pence is written in figures as £10-70. And last, two vertical lines running through the middle of the check have the effect of making the check valid for deposit only. It cannot be cashed, not by the person it is made out to, and not by a third party. Endorsing a check is not necessary for this simple reason; if it is made out to you, it can only be deposited in your account. The checking service is free as long as you maintain a minimum balance, which varies slightly with each bank.

The plastic **bank card** is a promise from the bank to cover your check up to an amount of 50 pounds, although you may make checks out for an amount above that. Be prepared to show your bank card when cashing checks in stores or other banks.

Ask to have your **bank statements** sent monthly rather than quarterly. Cancelled checks will not be returned to you.

A **savings account** is called a *deposit account*; a deposit into this account is called a *deposit account credit.*

Instead of safety-deposit boxes, banks have a **securities department** where you may leave your valuables for safekeeping. The system will at first strike you as being rather haphazard because they require you to furnish your own container, anything from a sealed envelope to a locked suitcase; they do not wish to know the contents; they state that they are not insured for the safety of the valuables; they do not give you a receipt; and there is only a nominal charge! Things are more official than they seem, however, and the Boxes and Parcels division is a good place to park your "stealables."

If you are a family operating in more than one currency, check with the bank manager for their **foreign currency services**. For instance, with a **same-day value account**, when you deposit a dollar check, you can use the money immediately, even though the check will take a good ten days to clear if drawn on a bank abroad.

Transferring money across banking and currency differences is easy, if not exactly fast. To transfer a dollar amount to the U.S. from your sterling account here, have the bank either draw a dollar check or a money order against your account here or, for a small charge, transfer dollar amounts by cable or telex. To transfer a dollar amount from your American account to your English sterling account, simply write a dollar check on your American account and deposit it here. Especially with larger amounts, however, the bank may wait to receive the dollars before crediting your account, and there will be a service charge.

Also look into the services and charges of a foreign currency account with one of the many American banks in London. The American Embassy's Consular Services will furnish you with a list.

Order ahead at your bank when you wish to buy actual foreign currency. Exchange rates, varying daily, are displayed on a notice board at the counter.

HOW TO PAY YOUR BILLS

There are many ways of paying your monthly bills. The most familiar to you, but not necessarily the most efficient, is to send a **check**. (Although the British spelling of *cheque* gives it a French air, the pronunciation remains the same.) You can avoid mailing costs and all that writing, however: simply collect the **giro slips** on the bottom of each bill, fill them in, take them in a pack to your bank, and write one check for the total amount. The bank will then pay the bills through the **Bank Giro Credit System.**

A similarly simple method is possible at any post office. If you have a bank account there (**Post Giro Account**) write your check against that account. Alternatively, you can pay the lump sum in cash and the post office will take care of it through **Transcash**. No postage or checks needed — just lots of cash!

You can also arrange to have your household bills paid without your direct involvement. Just instruct your bank to make a **standing order** or **direct debit payment**. They will then pay a specified amount to a specified payee at regular intervals — either a fixed amount or a varying amount, depending on the arrangement.

PLASTIC MONEY

There are two **bank credit cards**: Visa (including Barclaycard, issued by the bank of the same name, and Trustcard) and Access (part of Master Charge). There is no charge for receiving or using these cards, which are obtained from your bank. They allow you substantial credit and a lengthy period for payment.

There are two main **charge cards**: American Express and Diners Club. For big spenders (and big earners!) three Gold cards are available: American Express Gold, Barclays Premier, and Midland Gold.

BUILDING SOCIETIES

Building societies operate much like savings and loan associations in the U.S. Simply stated, they collect savings from the public and lend these to home-buyers. You can use either side of their services: when buying a house, take out a mortgage with them, and when saving, invest with them. Their interest rates tend to be higher than those of banks. Some of the major societies are Halifax Building Society, Anglia, Abbey National, Woolwich (say WOOLitch), Britannia, and Leicester (say LESter).

HOW TO TAKE YOUR MONEY TRAVELING

Any of the four **credit cards** mentioned above can be used when abroad. (Access is linked with Eurocard in Europe and Mastercard in the United States).

Four main types of **travelers checks** are available: American Express, Citicorp, Thomas Cook, and Visa. Building societies, post offices, and larger travel agents issue them, as well as banks.

Get a **Eurocheque encashment card** from your bank, which will allow you to use your regular bank checks abroad, made out in pounds sterling, at any bank displaying the red and blue EC symbol.

A few banks, Midland Bank among them, offer **Uniform Eurocheques** instead, a system long established in the rest of Europe. These special checks, along with an accompanying card, can be used at any bank (particularly in northern Europe) in the local currency. A card for use in automatic cash dispensers is also available from these same banks, but their use is so far confined mainly to Spain.

Postcheques are available to account holders with the National Girobank. With these you can withdraw cash in local currency from any post office abroad.

HOW TO PAY TAXES

Income Tax

One person who will welcome you warmly to England is Her Majesty's Inspector of Taxes. You will be expected, as you would anywhere, to part with a good share of your income to help defray public expenditure; the amount of your share will depend on two factors in addition to the size of your income — your **domicile** and your **resident status.**

Generally speaking, your **domicile** is the country which you regard as your natural and permanent home. Whether you are **resident** in England is determined by several factors, the most important of which is the length of your stay. As a rule, you can assume you are a resident in England for tax purposes if you reside here for more than six months out of a year. (In the following discussion it will be assumed that you and your spouse reside in England but that your domicile is outside England.)

As a **resident non-domiciled person**, you are liable to UK income tax on the following:

> income arising from UK sources, such as a job, a business, or investments in England; and

> income arising abroad and remitted to you in the UK.

Deductions are few and far between, job-related business expenses are deductible only to the extent that they are incurred wholly, exclusively, and necessarily in the course of your work. Medical expenses, property taxes, and other taxes are not deductible; interest paid on the first £30,000 of a mortgage on your house is deductible.

If **both husband and wife work**, they have the choice of being taxed separately on their salaries; it is usually advantageous to make this choice, unless the second salary is very low. A wife's income in the UK, other than salary (investment income, for example), is at all times added to her husband's income for tax purposes.

Pensions. If you plan to retire in England and you draw a pension from a pension fund outside England, this pension is taxed on a remittance basis. That is, if you do not have the pension remitted to you in the UK, it is not subject to UK taxes. Take care, though, because retiring in England may cause the transfer of your domicile to England, in which case you would become fully taxable on your worldwide income, including that pension.

Tax rates. Before tax is calculated, a personal exemption of about £3,200 (for a married couple) is deducted. The tax rate starts at 30% and reaches a maximum of 60% for incomes exceeding £38,500.

Remittances. As mentioned above, foreign income is taxable only if it is remitted to the UK; this means that the rent you receive for your house in your home country or the dividends from an overseas investment portfolio are not taxable as long as you keep them outside England. You can remit funds from abroad without having to pay part of them to the taxman, however, providing the remittance is made from money you already had before you moved to England or from funds received from non-income sources (such as loans, proceeds from the sale of investments, etc.) after you became a resident of the UK. You have to be careful, though, to keep these two non-taxable categories separate from "income," because if you remit money from an account which receives funds from both income and non-income sources, the Inland Revenue will assume that the income was remitted first.

A method often adopted to deal with this problem is the following: you open a second account with your bank in your home country, to be used exclusively for remittances to the UK. Of course this account will show an ever-increasing overdraft; however, banks are often willing to consider your two accounts as a unit in determining your overdraft position and in calculating interest.

Alternatively, you can use the first account to deposit all income and the second to receive all funds of a capital nature which are therefore not taxable in England, such as proceeds of investments sold, bond redemptions, and money borrowed. You must avoid transfer from the income account to the capital account; however, you may use the funds in the income account for expenses while you are outside England.

Rent. If you are renting a house in the UK, keep this in mind: you are required by law to withhold 30% tax from each payment and remit this to the Inland Revenue. If the rent is paid to an agent in the UK who is managing the property for the landlord, such as an estate agent, there is no obligation for you to withhold.

Capital Gains Tax. You will be liable to capital gains tax at a rate of 30% on profits over £5,900 on assets sold in the UK. The main exception to this rule is the profit realized on the sale of your principal residence and the land around it up to one acre; you do not have to pay capital gains tax on this amount.

The **Inspector of Taxes** responsible for your tax affairs will usually be located in the tax office dealing with your employer's tax matters. If you do not have a UK employer (for example, you have retired in the UK), then you should get in touch with the tax office of the district where you live. You can also take your questions to the following address:

Inland Revenue, General Enquiries Office
Somerset House, Strand
London WC2
tel. 01-438 6622

The **U.S. Internal Revenue Service** has advisers at the American Embassy, full-time during the tax season and part-time the rest of the year:

American Embassy
24 Grosvenor Square
London W1
tel. 01-499 9000

National Insurance Contributions. Your employer will deduct National Insurance Contributions from your salary under a variety of laws, including the National Health, amounting to some £1,200 a year.

Value-Added Tax (VAT) is levied at a rate of 15% on almost all goods and services sold. If you are exporting these goods within six months, you can claim back the VAT you paid.

CHAPTER 11

How To Use The Telephone

EMERGENCIES AND IMPORTANT NUMBERS

	Country Mouse	City Mouse (01 numbers)
Emergencies. Fire, police, and ambulance. Tell the operator which service you need.	999	999
Operator. She will connect you to Freefone numbers (toll-free, like 800 numbers), including Telecom's own numbers. Call her for a new telephone, inquiries about your phone bill, or any general problem, and she will connect you to the proper extension.	100	100
Directory inquiries (inland only)	192	142 (for London) 192 (other inland)
Operator service and inquiries to U.S. and Canada	155	107
Repair Service	151	151

Telegrams (inland only)	190	190
Telegrams (international only)	100	190
Telemessage (both in England and international)	100	190

THE TALKING PHONES: A SELECTION OF INTERESTING AND ENTERTAINING RECORDINGS

Time. The Speaking Clock is correct to the nearest twentieth of a second.

from London: 123
from Surrey and the south: 98081
other areas: check your *Telephone Dialling Codes* booklet.

Weather (for the London area). Telephone numbers for weather reports in other areas are listed in the back of your *Telephone Dialling Codes* booklet.

01-246 8091

Travel.	By rail	01-246 8030
	By road	01-246 8031
	By sea	01-246 8032
	By air	01-246 8033

London Transport   01-222 1234

Events in London   01-246 8041

Children's events in London   01-246 8007

Bedtime stories. Puffin Storyline from 6 p.m.; before that, you can hear your horoscope.   01-246 8000

Recipe. Provided daily by British Gas.   01-246 8071

Financial Times Index. Updated seven times daily, except weekends.   01-246 8026

THE TELEPHONE SYSTEM

The mere mention of the telephone system is enough to bring on a flood of frustrating stories — colorful descriptions of crossed lines, interrupted calls, and bad connections. British Telecom, the recently privatized company in charge, promises a brighter future, but until that happy day, you need to know three unusual but very basic facts in order to use the existing system.

First, the dialling code (local area code) for a local town depends on which town you are calling *from*. The solution is simple: you must consult the booklet called *Telephone Dialling Codes*. Keep a copy by each extension. The codes will be displayed in phone booths.

If you dial further afield than your local call area, the dialling code (sometimes called the area code or the STD code to distinguish it from codes for local calls) is always the same. Large cities always have the same dialling codes: London (01), Birmingham (02), Manchester (03).

To help people who want to call you, list your telephone number like this on your change-of-address cards or business stationery:

National: Byfleet (039 32) 46068
International: International prefix + 44 + (39 32) 46068

Second, your telephone bill will not be itemized. It will consist of two amounts; the first is the quarterly subscription fee and the second, a lump sum for all calls made (metered units), whether local, long distance, or international. If you wish to know more detail about your telephone charges, there are two not terribly satisfactory steps you can take: you can have a meter installed on your phone so that you can see the number of units being used (but this calls for bookkeeping on your part, since different units have different charges), or you can place your international calls via the operator, to have the charges itemized on your bill, but this increases the cost greatly.

Third, there is a charge for each and every call, depending on three things — length of call, distance, and time of day. Calls are charged as indicated by the charge letters in your *Telephone Dialling Codes* booklet; *L* is local and cheapest and includes all the towns listed in the first two pages of the booklet; *a* indicates up to 56 kilometers, and *b* over 56 kilometers.

Call charges for inland calls:
cheap rate 6 p.m. to 8 a.m., all weekend, and legal holidays
standard rate 8 a.m. to 9 a.m. and 1 p.m. to 6 p.m.
expensive rate 9 a.m. to 1 p.m.

INTERNATIONAL CALLS

International Direct Dialling (IDD) is possible to over 120 countries, about 93% of the world's telephones. In the back of the *Telephone Dialling Codes* booklet, you will find the country codes. A more complete listing of area codes is shown in the *International Telephone Guide,* available free by dialling 100 and asking for Freefone 2013. To make an international call, you need to dial.

International code → country code → area code → private number.

To dial other countries from England, first dial 010, which is the international code. Then dial the country code, which is 1 for both the U.S. and Canada.

To dial England from other countries, first dial the appropriate international code. Then dial 44, the country code for England; then dial the area code, dropping the initial zero.

The cheapest hours for international calls are from 8 p.m. to 8 a.m., Monday through Friday, and all weekend. In a burst of holiday spirit, British Telecom usually extends these at Christmastime, sometimes for as long as two weeks. Check the newspaper.

If you're confused about the telephone tones in other countries, call Freefone 2070 (for Europe) or Freefone 2071 (for North America) for a free demonstration.

The following reference library has the telephone books of business centers (i.e. large cities) throughout the world:

City Business Library (open during office hours)
Gillette House
55 Basinghall Street
London EC2
tel. 01-638 8215

DOMESTIC *(INLAND)* CALLS

Unfortunately, some telephone terminology seems to be as confusing as the telephone system itself. First of all, don't forget that there is a distinction between *calling* and *telephoning*. If you tell someone you'll call in an hour, they will expect to see you in person, so be sure to tell them you'll phone them or ring them.

A **long distance call** is a *trunk call*. (Question: What was the elephant doing in the phone booth? Answer: Making a trunk call!) A **collect call** is a *transferred charge call,* and a **person-to-person call** is a *personal call.* All of these must go through the operator and are available internationally. When you say you are on the telephone, it means you have a listed phone; if you have an unlisted number, you are *ex-directory*. If a line is busy, it is *engaged,* and you will hear an *engaged tone.*

You will have to develop a finely tuned musical ear to distinguish the various whirrs and burrs, beeps and peeps. There is the low, steady dial tone when you pick up the receiver, the frantic high-pitched tone demanding your coins in a phone booth, the slow beeps of the busy signal, and the somehow dead-sounding steady tone of an unsuccessful connection.

HOW TO USE A PAY PHONE *(CALL BOX, PUBLIC TELEPHONE, PHONE BOX, COIN BOX)*

If you're lucky enough to step into one of the rare booths with a Blue Pay Phone, just follow the instructions displayed in the digital display window. If not, the phone booth can be an adventure, with instructions like those for some quaint parlor game. The main thing to remember is that you must do all your dialling and someone must answer, before you insert any money. When the person called lifts up the receiver you will hear frantic beeps *(pips)* that will make you think you have made some mistake. Resist that impulse to hang up! This is the signal for you to insert your coins, and after a lot of clanking, you can talk for a limited period, after which the familiar beeps will signal you to insert more money. If you receive a call from a pay phone, the temptation to hang up when you hear those rapid beeps is just as strong. Don't do it! Give your caller time to insert the coins.

HOW TO SEND A TELEGRAM

Although British Telecom offers telegram service (see Emergencies and Important Numbers, at the beginning of this chapter), there is a thriving alternative telegram business. Some companies offer elaborate productions including exotic costumes and songs composed especially for the occasion. Others send singing telegrams anywhere in the world, charging according to travel expenses. Choose a Singing Telegram or a Kissogram, or make it as bizarre as you wish.

Songbird 01-286 8090

The American Telegram Company 01-351 4225

The Alternative Telegram Company 01-691 8826

HOW TO GET A FASHION PHONE

Telephone shops are opening all over. Although it seems to be perfectly legal to sell all these fashionable phones, it is definitely illegal to install any that do not have the approval of British Telecom. (They must have a tag on them with a red circle, warning you of this fact.) For information on legal fashion phones, call Freefone and ask for British Telecom's Sales Office, or go to one of the British Telecom shops in some department stores.

CHAPTER 12

How To Send It: Postal Services

THE POST OFFICE

At the post office you may be one of the few people doing anything as straightforward as buying stamps or mailing packages. At the window, great sums of money change hands (in both directions!), and complicated forms are passed back and forth. Besides local gossip you hear talk of licences, allowances, and benefits. Even if your post office is only a single window tucked away in the back of a stationery shop *(post office sub-station)*, it can help you with many transactions:

✥ **You can apply for a provisional drivers license and a driving test.** (See Chapter 9 on transportation for further details.)

✥ **You can pay for various licenses:** a **vehicle license** (for which you will receive a round sticker to display on the inside of your windshield), **a dog license** (cats run free), a **CB license,** a **hunting license,** and a **television license** (per house, not per set). Take your questions about your television license to

National Television Licence Records Office (NTVLRO)
Bristol BS98 1TL
tel. Bristol (0272) 48021

✥ **You can collect child benefits,** a gift to you from the Department of Health and Social Security for each child, to offset the lack of a tax deduction for children. Apply for it at the post office as soon as you arrive, although you cannot start collection until you have lived here six months, at which point it will be paid retroactively. Although only mothers can apply for this allowance, any designated person can collect it — either weekly, monthly, or quarterly.

♋ **You can open an account** with the post office's bank, the National Girobank, which offers the usual services of a regular bank. Use this account to pay the bills that have a giro slip attached.

♋ **You can pay monthly bills,** whether for telephone, electricity, water, gas, or credit card expenditures, with the giro slips attached to the bills. Tear them off and take the whole bundle either to the post office (use Giro Account or Transcash) or to the bank (use a single check). For further details, see Chapter 10 on money.

♋ **You can invest in National Savings Certificates and National Bonds** or open an Investment Account with the National Savings Bank, all offering competitive interest rates.

♋ **You can use Transcash,** similar to a postal order.

♋ **You can add to your stamp collection** by arranging for first-day covers. For information, write to the head office:
British Philatelic Bureau
FREEPOST
Edinburgh EH3 0HN

Membership for juniors is also available:
Stamp Bug Club
FREEPOST
High Wycombe
Bucks HP11 2TD

♋ **You can send flowers** from Flowerland, Ltd., at the New Covent Garden Market. Choose from six bouquets pictured in color on the brochure.

♋ **You can obtain a list of dentists and doctors in your area.**

The Royal Mail also carries out the mundane duties concerned with mail delivery. **Post office hours** are normally from 9:00 a.m. to 5:30 p.m. from Monday through Friday. Some offices open on Saturday morning from 9:00 a.m. until 12 noon; one of them, at King William IV Street near Trafalgar Square, is open 24 hours a day.

There are **two classes of letter mail.** First class carries a half-hearted promise of next-day delivery, and second class takes longer. If FREEPOST is part of the address, you don't need a stamp.

Address an envelope to a gentelman like this: Arnold E. Smith, Esq. (no Mr.). Write your return address on the back flap. **Address labels** are not easily available, so order them from

Abel-Label Department
Steelprint Ltd.
Earls Barton
Northampton NN6 01S

Don't forget to add the **postcode** after the name of the city or county. It is a combination of up to seven letters and numbers which identify your house and neighbors very specifically. For the Country Mouse, the first two letters denote the major sorting office (for example, KT denotes Kingston, GU denotes Guildford); for the City Mouse, the letters and numbers before the space denote a geographical area of London and correspond to the borough designations. (For example, the area of London known as SW7 also has that same designation at the beginning of its postcode.) The rest of the numbers and letters correspond to increasingly smaller geographical areas, so that in the end you may be the only one with that particular number. The police encourage you to mark your goods with this number for easier identification in the case of theft.

MAIL TO AND FROM FARAWAY PLACES

Count yourself fortunate if an airmail letter takes less than a week to reach North America. Deadlines for Christmas mail will be listed on the back page of the *Times* and in a booklet from the post office called *Overseas Christmas Mail.*

Although the day of red sealing wax has fortunately passed, the postman's critical eye will still examine your packages, so wrap them well. You may use a padded mailing envelope, available at post offices and stationery stores.

Receiving parcels from abroad can be an expensive experience because **duty** and **VAT** are due on each one unless it meets these three requirements:

It must be a gift sent by a private person.

The total value must not exceed £20 (if sent from a Common Market country, the limit is £40).

The goods must not be intended for commercial use.

Unless these conditions are met, you owe custom and excise duty (about 15%), Value Added Tax (also about 15%), and a handling charge on the full value of the contents.

You can ask the postal depot to hold the package while you complain about the custom and excise charges:

HM Customs and Excise
Kent House
Upper Ground
London SE1 9PS
tel. 01-626 1515

CHAPTER 13

Pubs

If you take your pub-crawling at all seriously, it won't be long before you've settled on a couple of favorites, your very subjective choices based on any one of the things that pubs offer: the coziness of a crackling fire and the low beams; a pint of the tastiest real ale around; the opportunity to mix with the colorful locals and hear their even more colorful stories; the welcoming family atmosphere lent by the adjoining playground; or the delicious "pub grub" that might include game soup and crusty bread.

Investigating pubs is a series of pleasant surprises. First of all, pub grub is inexpensive, hearty, and delicious. Try a **Ploughman's Lunch** (a hunk of cheese, fresh bread, and pickle on the side); a **jacket potato** (baked potato) with one of many toppings such as grated cheese, prawns, or meat; **Scotch Eggs** (hard-boiled eggs, surrounded by sausage meat, breaded and fried in oil until golden); **Toad-in-the-Hole** (a small sausage tucked under a blanket of Yorkshire Pudding batter); **Bangers and Mash** (sausage and mashed potatoes); or **Bubble and Squeak** (a casserole of mashed potatoes and cabbage that takes its name from the sounds it makes while cooking). Lighter lunches include an extensive salad bar, homemade soup, and an assortment of sandwiches. Many country pubs have proper restaurants in the back where you can dine at night on white tablecloths and enjoy some of the best food around.

You will be surprised at how easy it is to make pub-crawling a family activity. Although the law still technically prohibits children under 14 from entering a bar where alcohol is served, pubs eager for family trade get around this by setting aside a children's room, by allowing children in the beer garden, or by simply overlooking them. Of some 70,000 pubs, about half allow children.

Look around you for artistic surprises. The taps *(beer pumps)* at the bar, the cut-glass partitions (called *snob screens*), the low wooden beams, and the pub signs are often works of art.

You may also be surprised at the variety of beers. Until now, beer to you has probably meant a pale yellow brew served ice-cold in a modest glass. This is known here as *a half pint of lager* and is only for the timid or, some would say, for the ladies.

Consider, instead, these alternatives to your bland brew: order a pint of **real ale**, beer that has been matured naturally in its own cask and is pumped to the bar from below or tapped directly from the cask. It will be served only slightly below room temperature, to enhance the flavor. (Guinness, for example, is ideally served at 58 degrees.) There is no foam *(froth)* because the pint glass itself is a legal measure when filled to the brim, and any foam would take away from the legal amount in the standard pint. (Examine your glass to find a stamp from the Weights and Measures Department.) Thanks to the efforts of an organization called CAMRA (Campaign for Real Ale), whose members scorn the half-pint lager drinkers, more and more pubs are offering this tasty, natural beer.

Or order a pint of **bitter**, considered the typical English beer. The taste is surprisingly light in contrast to its somber color and unappetizing name.

Be even more adventuresome and order **Guinness**, bottled **stout**, with a real head of foam, the only exception to the no-foam rule. (In a special court ruling, it was decided that foam was an integral part of Guinness and therefore allowable, as long as it didn't exceed 3/8 of an inch!) Add champagne to your Guinness for a wicked drink called Black Velvet.

Just about the only unpleasant surprise for the pub-crawler is opening hours. These are irregular and depend on the geographical area, the day of the week, and the whim of the proprietor. Pubs are allowed to open for a maximum of 9½ hours a day, with a break of at least two hours in the afternoon. You can expect something like this: 11:30 a.m. – 2:30 p.m. and 5:30 p.m. – 10:30 p.m. Hours on Sunday are standard (and more miserly): from 12 – 2 and 7 – 10:30 p.m. We have a teetotaler, Lloyd George, to thank for this disruption of our drinking habits. He instigated these restrictions during the First World War in an attempt to control the most popular leisure-time activity of his munitions workers, and we're still stuck with them, some 70 years later.

Etiquette in a pub is just as informal as you'd expect, but here are some tips to make you as inconspicuous as a regular, even on your first visit: after entering the door marked *saloon* (the door marked *public* is for shirt-sleeved regulars), order your drink at the bar and pay for it right then (no tipping). Order your food from another part of the bar (maybe even in another room) and pay for it then (no tipping). Find a table. When your warm food is ready, your number will be called (especially if you're in the garden) and you pick it up yourself. It is customary for each person to treat the others in his group to a round of beer. You will hear it said that "three men in a pub equals three rounds of beer."

For a complete listing of pubs, with detailed descriptions, read *The Good Pub Guide* by Alisdair Aird, published by the Consumers' Association.

For advice on particular pubs, call one of these numbers:

Pub Information Bureau — tel. 01-837 7733

Pub Information Centre — tel. 01-222 3232

Pub & Restaurant Information Bureau — tel. 01-907 4600

The pubs below deserve Mouse Mention. While highly subjective, this list will serve as a starting point for your pub-crawling.

Coziest Garden
The Withies
Compton, Surrey (just south of Guildford)

Most Colorful History (an ancient smugglers' inn)
Mermaid
Rye, Sussex
tel. Rye (07973) 3065 (rooms available)

Most Artistic Pub Sign, Oldest Pub, Best Playground
    Equipment
White Hart
Witley, Surrey (south of Guildford, on the A283)

Lowest Beams
Cricketers
Downside Common
Cobham, Surrey

Longest Bar Counter
Holborn Bars
22 High Holborn
London WC1

 Prettiest Snob Screens
Lamb
94 Lamb's Conduit Street
London WC1

 Prettiest Village
White Horse
Shere, Surrey

 Best Location for Antique Shopping
Anchor
Ripley, Surrey

 Closest American Historical Ties (Pilgrim Fathers set sail
    from here.)
Mayflower
117 Rotherhithe Street
London SE16

 Most Impressive View (of St. Paul's Cathedral)
Founders Arms
Bankside
. London SE1

 Best Home Brew
Goose & Firkin (and four other Firkin pubs)
47 Borough Road
London SE1

CHAPTER 14

Cultural Highlights: How To Enjoy the Theater

A stroll through London's theater district might well remind you of a well-stocked bookshop — there seems to be something to satisfy every taste. There's the comedy that leaves you with your sides aching with laughter, the long-running favorite for which you can just make the 13,000th performance, the musical that sets you humming, and the serious drama that sparks an earnest discussion with your after-theater dinner partner. In London there are some 50 theaters within an area of about two square miles known as the **West End**, and most of the plays you attend will be in this area, concentrated around The Strand, Covent Garden, St. Martins Lane, Charing Cross Road, and Shaftesbury Avenue. But don't neglect the theater that thrives outside the West End: the **fringe theater** (Roundhouse, ICA Theatre, and Kings Head Theatre Club); **local theaters** which may offer trial runs for West End productions (Hampstead Theatre, Greenwich Theatre, and Lyric Studio in Hammersmith); **suburban theaters** which offer traditional fare (Wimbledon Theatre, Richmond Theatre, and Yvonne Arnaud Theatre in Guildford); **theater for children** (Young Vic, Shaw Theatre, Polka Theatre in Wimbledon); and **lunch-time performances** on a small noncommercial scale.

HOW TO FIND OUT WHAT'S PLAYING

All West End plays are listed in your daily newspaper. Some alternative theater is mentioned there, but for the most complete listings get a weekly copy of either *Time Out* or *What's On*. For a pleasant surprise each Thursday morning, arrange to have your newsagent deliver *Time Out* tucked into your daily newspaper.

Have your name put on the theater mailing lists for a nominal fee. This is possible for the National Theatre, the Royal Shakespeare Company in Stratford and at the Barbican in London, The Royal Festival Hall, The Royal Opera House, and the English National Opera at the London Coliseum. If you become a Friend of Covent Garden, a more expensive decision, you will receive special booking privileges at these last two theaters, information about lectures and advance programs, and tours of the theaters. Expand your circle of Friends in this way to include not only Covent Garden but also the Royal Academy, the Tate Gallery, and other art institutions — friendship for a fee that benefits all concerned.

Another way to discover what's playing: Inquire at a *theater ticket agency,* either by phone or in person. The main ones include Keith Prowse & Co., Thomas Cook, and Edwards & Edwards. Check the Yellow Pages under the heading *Theatre Ticket Agencies* for a listing of their branches. Some are located in main department stores.

HOW TO GET THEATER TICKETS

Use your credit card by calling the special telephone number given with the individual theater listings. Look for the letters *cc*. You don't need to pick the tickets up until just before the performance; your pre-paid tickets will be waiting for you at the box office. You can also have them sent for an additional charge, time permitting.

Go to the box office in person. Most box offices are open six days a week, except Sunday (when there is no performance). The inconvenience of getting there will be offset by the fact that you will get a more accurate idea of the location of the seats — and you will have the tickets in your pocket.

Use a ticket agency located in department stores, travel agencies, and individual shops in London. Prices are higher, but on the other hand, this is often the only place to get tickets for popular shows that are in great demand. Go in person, or if you have an account at the store where a ticket agency is located, just phone them; the tickets will be sent to you and charged to your store account.

Book by mail *(postal booking)* by writing to the theater well in advance, giving your choice of seats and enclosing a check (preferably left blank, with an upper limit suggested) and a stamped self-addressed envelope. Tickets will be sent to you.

Go to the green-and-white ticket booth at Leicester Square, organized by SWET, the Society of West End Theatres. It is open from 2:30 to 6:30 and on matinee days from noon. Here you can buy half-price tickets for some shows for the same day. The line often stretches halfway around the square, so get there early and bring an umbrella.

Tickets for most fringe theaters are available from the Fringe Box Office:

Duke of York's Theatre
St. Martin's Lane
London WC2
tel. 01-379 6002 (credit card booking)

Canceling tickets is a delicate business. If you notify the theater well in advance, and if they are able to resell the tickets, they will allow you to change your booking to another time. Chances are slim that your money will be refunded.

TYPES OF SEATING

There are usually three or four different prices of seats in any auditorium. Remember that most theaters are so small that there is hardly a bad seat in the house.

Stalls on the ground floor are the most expensive.

Dress circle is the first balcony; its first rows are often as expensive (and desirable) as the stalls.

Upper circle is the second balcony.

Balcony is farthest away.

Box seats, clinging to the side of the auditorium, offer intimacy but a rather skewed view of the stage.

TIPS FOR AN EVENING AT THE THEATER

Box offices are open six days a week, except Sunday, usually from 10 a.m. to 8 p.m.

Drinks for the intermission *(interval)* may be ordered and paid for before the performance starts, to avoid the crush at the bar.

Food at the theater can range from a gourmet spread to cheap snack food. Almost all theaters will have ice cream for intermission, but for the ultimate in theater munching, take along your own box of chocolates. Etiquette allows you and your seat mates to consume the whole box during intermission!

At Christmastime, attend a **pantomime**, a play based on a fairy tale, with bawdy songs and racy humor. The leading parts are played by actors of the opposite sex, so Cinderella is a man and Prince Charming a girl in tights! This is excellent family entertainment, with lots of silliness; the worst of the naughty jokes will pass over most children's heads.

Performances usually take place six days a week, except Sunday, with two matinees. Try the Saturday matinee, usually at a very civilized 5 o'clock, and then still feel wide awake enough to enjoy dinner afterwards.

Previews are given prior to opening nights for several performances, usually at reduced prices.

Smoking is never permitted in the auditorium.

Theater tours are available for many theaters:
Theatreland Tours
10 St. Martin's Court
London, WC2
tel. 01-240 0915

SPECIAL THEATERS

Four **special theaters** deserve mention and your special attention because of the extent of their activities and the nature of their performances: The National Theatre, The Barbican Centre, The Royal Shakespeare Company, and the Open Air Theatre.

The National Theatre

The National Theatre can be found in the modern complex of buildings that dominate the South Bank of the Thames. In contrast to the functional unimaginative buildings, the entertainment inside is creative and varied. You can take a romantic river walk; have a snack on the terrace overlooking the river; eat in one of the restaurants, bars, or buffets; shop for books and records in their bookshop; listen to excellent music in the foyer; take a guided tour of the buildings; and admire free art exhibitions.

Besides all this, you can attend one of the three excellent theaters: the **Olivier** with its open stage and fan-shaped auditorium, named for Sir Lawrence Olivier; the **Lyttleton** with a conventional proscenium stage; and the **Cottesloe**, the smallest of the three. If you're lucky, half-price tickets will be available in the lobby before performances.

> The National Theatre
> South Bank
> London SE1
> tel. 01-928 2252
>   01-928 3052 (credit card booking)
>   01-928 8126 (24-hour recorded booking information)

Because plays are in repertory, you need to be put on the NT mailing list. For a schedule and for booking forms, call them or send a stamped self-addressed envelope:

> NT Mailing List
> FREEPOST
> London SE1
> tel. 01-928 2033, ext. 319

Eat dinner overlooking the Thames before or after the performance, from 5:30 p.m. to 12:30 a.m. For table reservations, call 01-928 2033, ext. 531 (during the day) or ext. 561 (evenings).

The Barbican Centre

The Barbican Centre, an art complex, is the home of the Royal Shakespeare Company and the London Symphony Orchestra and the site of many cultural events: art exhibits, chamber music concerts, children's films, plays, and orchestral concerts. It also has two lending libraries. For complete information, have your name added to their mailing list.

> The Barbican Centre
> Silk Street
> London EC2
> tel. 01-628 8795
>   01-638 8891 (credit card booking)
>   01-588 7733 (mailing list)
>   01-638 4141 (Children's Cinema Club)

The Royal Shakespeare Company

The Royal Shakespeare Company performs in London and in Stratford-upon-Avon (and in Vienna, Madrid, Prague, New York, and Barcelona, to mention just a few). The Stratford season, lasting from mid-March to October, is very popular and quickly sold out. Join the RSC mailing list by sending them a stamped self-addressed envelope:

> Royal Shakespeare Company, Mailing List
> Stratford-upon-Avon, Warwickshire CV37 6BB
> tel. Stratford (0789) 295623
>   Stratford (0789) 67262 (for special offers that include meals
>   and hotel accommodations with your play tickets.)

The Open Air Theatre

During the summer season, the months of June, July, and August, you can attend the Open Air Theatre. Regent's Park is a lovely setting for lunchtime plays, Sunday concerts, and performances by the New Shakespeare Company. Bring your own flask of warming drink.

Open Air Theatre
Regent's Park, Inner Circle
London NW1
tel. 01-486 2431

OUTER LONDON THEATERS

These three theaters are on the fringe — but only geographically, not artistically. Some plays are being tested before heading for the West End, but most are old favorites for audiences who like their art in familiar form. Check your local newspapers and the notice board of the larger libraries in your area to find out the schedules of the theaters listed below and also of the theaters in Farnham, Leatherhead, and Windsor.

The Richmond Theatre
The Green
Richmond, Surrey
tel. 01-940 0088

The Wimbledon Theatre
The Broadway
London (Wimbledon) SW19
tel. 01-542 2883

Yvonne Arnaud Theatre (say EEvon ARno)
Millbrook
Guildford, Surrey
tel. Guildford (0483) 64571

OPERA AND DANCE PERFORMANCES

Covent Garden, where Eliza Doolittle once sold a bunch of flowers to Henry Higgins, still has a cultural feeling to it, particularly in the evenings as people wander about in evening dress. They are headed not only for the many small theaters in the area and the Theatre Royal in Drury Lane, where most stage musicals are performed, but also for the elegant **Royal Opera House.** It is the home of the Royal Ballet Company and the site of many grand opera performances. It is sumptuous and elegant!

Royal Opera House
Covent Garden
London WC2
tel. 01-240 1066
   01-836 6903 (credit card booking)

The **London Coliseum** is the home of the English National Opera. Look up to see the globe on top of the building, flashing with lights:

London Coliseum Theatre
St. Martin's Lane
London WC2
tel. 01-836 3161
   01-240 5258 (credit card booking)

CONCERT HALLS

The **South Bank Arts Centre** has three concert halls: the Royal Festival Hall (which can accommodate almost 3,000 people), the Queen Elizabeth Hall (which seats about 1,000) and the Purcell Room (for chamber music groups and single performers). For a nominal fee, their mailing list department will send you the monthly schedules.

South Bank Concert Halls
Belvedere Road
London SE1
tel. 01-928 3191

The **National Film Theatre** also resides here. To see the

noncommercial films they show, you must become a member. Contact them for further information: 01-928 3232.

The **Royal Albert Hall**, named for Queen Victoria's beloved husband, is the site of the annual concerts known as *The Proms*. It is also used for such varied things as political gatherings, tennis tournaments, banquets, and exhibitions.

Royal Albert Hall
Kensington Gore
London SW7
tel. 01-589 8212

Wigmore Hall, created by Bechstein of grand piano fame, is elegant, decorated with marble and alabaster. It is used mainly for chamber music and solo recitals.

Wigmore Hall
Wigmore Street
London W1
tel. 01-935 2141

Sutton Place, near Guildford in Surrey, was built in 1530 and visited by King Henry VIII only three years later. They now offer various concert programs, all of them in the elegant Great Hall and some of them with dinner or tea afterward. For information and tickets, contact the Bookings Manager:

Sutton Place
Guildford, Surrey GU4 7QV
tel. Guildford (0483) 504455

FURTHER INFORMATION ON MAJOR EVENTS

Other events in London, too numerous to discuss here, are listed in the **London Log**, a two-page pamphlet that lists major events by month for the whole year. The London Tourist Board publishes it and you can obtain your free copy from them or from other tourist centers:

London Tourist Board
26 Grosvenor Gardens
London SW1
tel. 01-730 0791 (information)
tel. 01-246 8041 (recorded service, a selection of the main
   events of the day in and around London)

Write your own notes below.

MOUSE NOTES

Write your own notes below.

164

Index

Travel. *See* Transportation
  Travel information, 138

V

VAT, 136
Vegetables, 100
  Pick-your-own farms, 99
Viewing a house, 18-20

U

Underground, 122-123
University information, 34, 40-41, 42.
  See also Adult education

W

Weight, chart, 85
Which?, 54, 66, 118
Work permit, 45